BEYOND UNDERSTANDING

PEACE OF MIND IN THE HEART OF GOD

TIERRE FORD

Copyright 2025 © By Tierre Ford
All rights reserved. No parts of this book may be reproduced or transmitted in any form or by any means electronic or mechanical without permission in writing from publisher

ABOUT THE AUTHOR

At just 12 years old, I started selling drugs in the 6th grade—following the blueprint I saw in my own home. My father was both a dealer and a user, and by the 7th grade, I had bought my first car, was paying my mama rent, and buying my own school clothes.

That same year, the school system labeled me as "slow." They placed me in a remedial reading class—embarrassed me, honestly. I was ashamed. But I still kept my swag, my gold chains, my Starter jackets, and my game face. I was one of the most popular kids in school, but truth be told, I had stopped learning. I was only there to show off.

Then one day, my reading teacher—who I'll never forget—looked me in my eyes and said, "You don't belong in this class. You're smart. Don't let them label you." Her words stuck with me, even though my CRT test scores said otherwise.

At age 12 years old I became my neighborhood's youngest drug supplier. I started with 10 dollars, and I flipped that all the way to over $500,000. Me and my Dad link up dealing together supplying the market. I dropped out of high school in the 10th grade. I bought my mother a house with a pool in the backyard, purchased luxury cars, before I was locked up at 19.

At that point in my life, I had never read a full book. Not one. But my father always told me, **"The mind is the most powerful tool in the universe. Street sense and book sense together? That's unstoppable."**

So I gave books a chance.

It started with street fiction. Then history. Then business. Then biographies about powerful and wealthy people. I started seeing myself in those pages—not always in their polish, but in their ambition, their boldness. Then I read **Think and Grow Rich and As a Man Thinketh.** Those two books changed my entire mindset.

That's when I met my friend Cool Harris. I saw some of his writing on a notepad, and it rocked my world. I realized I had something to say, too. From that moment on, I picked up the pencil—and I've never looked back.

I earned my GED, took business and college courses, and started studying resilience. I discovered that, back in the day, Black people were once forbidden to read. There's even a saying: **"If you want to hide something from a Black person, put it in a book."** That became my fuel.

Now, I write both fiction and self-help books, covering everything from mindset and mental toughness to financial strategy and spiritual growth. I pour my soul into every page with one mission: to light a fire inside someone who's ready for change.

To everyone who's followed my journey—thank you. Let's set the world on fire with truth, with courage, with knowledge. Let's break every chain and every myth that says we don't read.

Peace—And Keep The Faith.

TIERRE FORD

SYNOPSIS

In a world that constantly pulls us outward—into fear, stress, uncertainty, and noise—**Peace Beyond Understanding** is a sacred return inward. This transformative book is not just a guide; it's a healing companion, a spiritual mirror, and a soul's roadmap back to the center.

Blending timeless wisdom with deeply personal insight, *Peace Beyond Understanding* offers 57 chapters of reflection, meditation, and practice drawn from ancient teachings, spiritual traditions, and heart-led truths. You'll journey through themes like:

- **Stress as a Messenger** (not a master)
- **Meditation beyond the Mind**
- **Affirmations that Rebuild the Soul**
- **Healing the Inner Child**
- **Breaking Generational Curses**
- **Love as Law**
- **Presence: The Only Place God Lives**
- **Living as Light**
- **Surrender Is Not Defeat**
- **The Return to Wholeness**
- **Beyond the Mind, Into the Heart of God**

Each chapter stands alone yet builds toward a powerful whole: a spiritual awakening that teaches peace is not the absence of problems—it's the presence of divine perspective.

You'll learn how to turn emotional pain into spiritual power, create sacred space in everyday life, move through your triggers with breath and grace, and build a quiet strength that no storm can shake.

Whether you're healing from the past, searching for deeper meaning, or simply trying to stay anchored in a chaotic world, *Peace Beyond Understanding* meets you where you are—and gently leads you home.

ould you like a shorter version for the back of the book or Amazon description?

1

THE COUSINS OF CHAOS: FEAR, DOUBT, STRESS, AND UNCERTAINTY

There is a storm that never makes the news. It doesn't flood streets or burn forests, but it consumes people all the same. It arrives in whispers—in the sleepless hours of the night, in the shallow breath before a big decision, in the numb stillness when the future feels too uncertain to touch. Its name is not one, but four: fear, doubt, stress, and uncertainty. Cousins, not by blood, but by spiritual affliction. They enter without knocking, and once inside, they rearrange the furniture of the soul.

Fear is often the first to arrive. It wears many masks: fear of failure, fear of loss, fear of rejection, fear of death. Fear's power lies in its ability to paralyze the present with imagined futures. It doesn't need truth to be loud; it only needs belief. Doubt follows close behind, a quiet saboteur. Doubt doesn't scream, it whispers. It asks questions with thorns: Are you sure? What if you can't? What if they leave? Doubt doesn't destroy you directly—it makes you do it to yourself.

Stress, then, is the natural consequence. A body wired for survival begins to break under the weight of invisible battles. Stress shows up in the neck, in the gut, in the mind that can't stop spinning. We drink it down with coffee, try to bury it in to-do lists, or sweat it out at the gym. But it waits. And uncertainty—the final cousin—lingers like fog. It makes you second-guess every step, trust no outcome, and live in a constant state of contingency.

Together, they form a cycle. One fuels the next. Fear gives birth to doubt, which breeds stress, which deepens uncertainty, which feeds fear once again. And around we go. A wheel of discontent powered by the lies our thoughts tell when they forget their Source.

But what if we paused? What if we asked the simplest question: where do these voices come from?

Not every voice in your mind deserves a microphone.

We must learn to recognize when thoughts are not facts. Fear is not prophecy. Doubt is not discernment. Stress is not strength. And uncertainty is not always danger. These are signals, not truths. Flags waving from the edges of consciousness asking for one thing: presence.

In spiritual teachings across traditions, we find a common invitation: "Be still."

In the Bible, Psalms 46:10 says, "Be still and know that I am God." In the Bhagavad Gita, Lord Krishna says, "Perform your duty and leave the rest to me." In Buddhism, mindfulness is the art of noticing without judgment. The Tao Te Ching whispers, "Do you have the patience to wait until your mud settles and the water is clear?"

Stillness is not inaction. It is a spiritual posture. It is the space where healing begins.

To confront fear, you must step into the present. Not the imagined catastrophe of tomorrow, not the regret of yesterday. Now. Right now. The breath in your lungs is your anchor. Each inhale is a reminder: I am alive. Each exhale, a declaration: I let go.

Doubt can only survive in silence. Speak life into yourself. Affirm what is good. Speak scripture, speak truth, speak declarations rooted in love. Words carry frequency. When you speak healing, your cells respond. Your spirit realigns.

Stress demands boundaries. It thrives in chaos. Simplify. Clean your physical space. Unplug from the false urgency of screens. Reclaim your morning with prayer, meditation, silence. Protect your peace like it's gold—because it is.

And uncertainty? It is a spiritual gift in disguise. For what is faith if not the courage to walk forward when you do not know what lies ahead? Uncertainty is the birthplace of miracles. It is the womb of new beginnings. Instead of fearing it, bless it. Say aloud: "I do not know what comes next, but I trust it is for my highest good."

Our ancestors faced trials without therapists, podcasts, or planners. They sat by a firelight and looked to the stars. They trusted the soil to yield. They knew storms passed, and seasons changed. And they told stories. Stories that reminded them: *You are not alone. You are not weak. You are not stuck.*

Today, we need new stories.

Stories that speak healing into broken minds. Stories that remind us: You are not your past. You are not your fear. You are not your worst day. You are not what they said about you in anger. You are not what trauma tried to make you become.

You are light wrapped in skin. You are breath borrowed from the Eternal. You are the prayer of someone who came before you. You are the proof that peace can exist after pain.

But to live in this peace, we must become aware. Awareness is the light switch in a dark room. It doesn't change the furniture, but it lets you see what's there. Once you see it, you can move it. You can cleanse the space. You can make it sacred again.

When fear rises, sit with it. Ask: What are you trying to protect? When doubt creeps in, ask: What would I do if I trusted myself fully? When stress overwhelms, ask: What must I release that was never mine to carry? When uncertainty freezes you, whisper: What is the next loving step I can take?

This is not perfection. This is practice. Peace of mind doesn't arrive like a package on your doorstep. It is cultivated, moment by moment, breath by breath, truth by truth.

And here is a truth you must never forget: It shall pass.

This moment. This ache. This fear. It is not eternal. But you are.

Peace beyond understanding does not come from having answers. It comes from living in trust.

In the next chapters, we will explore practices, teachings, and ancient truths that help reclaim this peace. But for now, let today be a sacred beginning. Look in the mirror. See the survivor. See the seeker. See the soul.

You have made it here. You have breath. You have a choice. You are already enough.

Close your eyes. Put your hand over your heart. Feel the rhythm. That is your proof.

Let it be known in the heavens and the earth: Peace is not far. Peace is already within.

Welcome to your healing.

Narrator's Reflection: We often believe that peace must be earned, that it arrives only when our lives are polished and presentable. But the deepest peace comes not from perfection, but from presence. In the muddy, messy middle of life—in the cries, in the questions, in the moments that make no sense—there is stillness waiting to be discovered. Peace does not mean the absence of fear; it means fear no longer controls the room. And today, that peace is calling you by name.

2

THE WORDS THAT WOUND: HOW LANGUAGE TRIGGERS THE SPIRIT

There are phrases that live in us longer than we realize. Words spoken in anger, sarcasm, or indifference that lodged themselves deep into the psyche. And while bones may heal and bruises fade, words often echo. A single sentence, delivered at the wrong time, can become a life sentence in the mind of a wounded soul.

"You're not good enough." "Why can't you be more like them?" "No one will ever want someone like you." "You're too much."

We may have heard these words from parents, teachers, lovers, or ourselves. Regardless of the source, they shape us. And if not challenged, they define us.

In spiritual traditions across time, words are treated not casually, but sacredly. In the Book of Genesis, God creates the world with words: "Let there be light." In John 1:1, it declares, "In the beginning was the Word, and the Word was with God, and the

Word was God." In the Dhammapada, the Buddha says, "What we think, we become. What we feel, we attract. What we imagine, we create."

Words are not just sounds. They are seeds. They create inner landscapes.

If someone speaks rain into your soul every day, you will grow in the shape of clouds. If someone pours light, you bloom.

This chapter is about learning to *hear* again. Not with your ears—but with your spirit.

Every word you allow to live inside you must be inspected. Was it spoken in love? Was it spoken in truth? Does it bring you closer to peace, or closer to fear?

One of the most powerful practices of spiritual healing is rewording your inner world. Rewriting the inner script.

You may have been told you were worthless. Today, say aloud: "I am worthy. I was created with intention." You may have been told you would fail. Say instead: "Every failure is fertilizer. I grow because I try." You may have told yourself you were broken. Replace it with: "I am healing. I am becoming whole."

Affirmations are not fluff. They are frequency. Your nervous system listens to your language. If you keep saying, "I'm so stupid," it responds accordingly. If you say, "I am learning," it aligns differently. There is no magic in the words themselves—the power is in your alignment.

We must also take responsibility for the words we speak to others. Healing is not just personal, it is relational.

How many children walk around carrying invisible wounds because of words their parents don't even remember saying? How many relationships unravel because apologies were withheld and kind words were rationed like gold?

Your tongue is a tool. It can be a balm or a blade.

Speak with care. Speak with truth. Speak with softness where needed, firmness where necessary.

And when others speak harm to you, remember: You can return it to the sender.

Not every word deserves a home inside your heart. Not every opinion is an oracle.

Choose what you plant. Choose what you water. Choose what you grow.

Narrator's Reflection: Language is spiritual technology. The words we whisper in private shape the worlds we build in public. We heal not only by hearing love, but by speaking it—to ourselves and others. This chapter invites you to check your inner vocabulary. Are your words building peace? Or burning bridges? If you want a new life, begin with a new language. Because peace begins with what you tell yourself when no one else is around.

3

THE FALSE SECURITY OF CONTROL

Control is the illusion we cling to when chaos seems too big to face. It whispers to us that if we just plan better, hold tighter, predict more accurately, we can keep pain at bay. We build schedules, create backup plans, micromanage outcomes, and try to steer every conversation, relationship, and situation toward our preferred result. But the tighter we grip, the more peace slips through our fingers.

The desire for control isn't inherently evil. It's a protective instinct. Somewhere deep inside, many of us learned that to be safe, we had to anticipate the worst. Some of us were children in volatile homes, learning to read the emotional weather of a room. Others were betrayed by people or life events that taught us: if you don't control things, you'll get hurt.

But spiritual peace requires the opposite. It demands surrender.

Not surrender as in giving up. Surrender as in letting go of the illusion that you were ever in charge of the outcome in the first place. Control is not the same as power. Power is rooted in divine truth. Control is rooted in fear.

Think of the ocean. You cannot control the tide. But you can learn to swim. You can learn to float. You can ride the waves instead of resisting them.

In Christianity, Jesus spoke of relinquishing worry by trusting the Father: "Therefore do not worry about tomorrow, for tomorrow will worry about itself. Each day has enough trouble of its own." (Matthew 6:34)

In Taoism, the principle of Wu Wei teaches the art of non-doing—not passivity, but acting in alignment with the natural flow of life. In Islam, the word "Islam" itself means surrender to the will of God. In Buddhism, attachment to control is a root cause of suffering. In all traditions, peace and surrender walk hand in hand.

So how do we begin to loosen the grip?

First, we identify where control is masking fear. Do you obsessively plan your future out of a fear of failure? Do you micromanage your relationships to avoid abandonment? Do you struggle to delegate because trust feels unsafe?

Second, we practice small surrenders. Let someone else drive. Leave a day unscheduled. Pray or meditate in silence without asking for anything. Observe how your nervous system reacts. Observe how your ego protests.

Third, we begin to trust that peace is not something we control—it's something we allow.

There is no amount of overthinking that can make life completely predictable. There is no checklist that can stop all pain. There is no plan B for destiny.

The soul does not thrive in cages, even if those cages are made of calendars and color-coded charts.

We must learn to live in the holy tension of doing our best and letting go. This is the true spiritual practice: disciplined effort paired with open hands.

You show up. You plant. You water. And you trust the sun to rise.

Control demands guarantees. Faith celebrates mysteries.

Your peace is not dependent on having every detail figured out. It is found in knowing that whatever happens—you will not be alone, and you will not be undone.

Narrator's Reflection: Letting go of control feels like falling, until you realize you were never standing on solid ground to begin with. Control is a coping mechanism, but surrender is a sacred strategy. To trust life, to trust God, to trust that your future doesn't require your obsession—this is where peace blooms. Not in the rigidity of control, but in the rhythm of trust. Today, ask yourself: Where am I holding too tightly? And what would happen if I let go with love?

4

ECHOES FROM EDEN: ORIGINAL PEACE LOST

Before the chaos, there was harmony. Before the fall, there was Eden. Whether taken as a literal garden or a metaphor for divine alignment, Eden represents a time when humanity was in sync with the Source—walking in step with the Divine, unashamed, unafraid, and fully present.

In that state, there was no striving. No anxiety. No scarcity. The presence of God was not a distant hope, but a felt reality. Peace was not something to be earned—it was the natural atmosphere.

And then came separation.

The moment Adam and Eve reached for the fruit, they weren't just breaking a rule; they were believing a lie: that they were not enough without more. That they had to *do* something to *become* something.

That belief still lives in us.

In every temptation to overwork. In every moment we hustle for love. In every thought that says, "If only I had this, then I'd be okay."

The expulsion from Eden wasn't just geographical. It was psychological. A break from union with God. A fracture in the soul's memory. Ever since, we have been trying to get back to that place of peace—often looking in all the wrong directions.

We search for Eden in relationships, promotions, money, followers, status, likes, luxury. But peace isn't in any of those things. Peace is a return. A remembering.

You were not created for chaos. You were not born to live in constant anxiety. The pulse of peace still lives inside you.

That is the echo.

All spiritual teachings at their core point back to that garden. Back to oneness. Back to presence. Back to love without shame, security without striving.

In Sufism, the mystical branch of Islam, they speak of *fana*—the annihilation of the self so that only God remains. In Christianity, the veil in the temple was torn so that the Divine could dwell within us again. In Hinduism, the *atman* is recognized as a spark of Brahman—divine essence clothed in flesh. And in Buddhism, enlightenment is the realization that suffering ends when illusion ends.

The illusion is that peace is something we lost. The truth is: peace is something we forgot.

The journey of healing is not about becoming something new. It's about peeling away everything that is not truly you.

Who were you before the trauma? Before the disappointments? Before the labels?

That is the you God still sees. That is you that hears Eden whispering.

When you sit in silence long enough, you can hear it: The memory of wholeness. The sound of breath syncing with eternity. The heartbeat that says, "You are loved. You are seen. You are safe."

You don't have to earn your return. You only have to accept it.

Repentance is not just about guilt. It's about changing direction. Turning back toward peace.

Let today be a homecoming. Not to a place. But to a presence.

Sit still. Close your eyes. Breathe. And listen.

The garden is not gone. It lives inside you.

Narrator's Reflection: All longing is homesickness for the soul's original peace. The world teaches us to look outward, to chase, to earn, to climb. But the Kingdom of God is within. Your truest identity is not the one shaped by fear, trauma, or achievement. It is the child walking barefoot in the garden, naked yet unashamed. That part of you is still alive. Still reachable. Still waiting for you to remember. Eden is not lost. Eden is waiting for your next breath.

5

THE WAR IN THE MIND: DUALITY AND THE EGO

If Eden was the garden of unity, then the mind—left unchecked—is the battlefield of duality. It is here where peace is often lost, not to war outside, but to war within. The ego, which once served as a simple interface between spirit and body, has become for many a tyrant. Loud, insecure, always grasping, always comparing. Its mantra is separation. Its mission is self-preservation at all costs.

The ego says: "I am not safe unless I'm superior." The ego says: "They have more, so I must lack." The ego says: "If I admit weakness, I will be destroyed."

And so we armor up. We build identities made of performance. We speak from pride instead of truth. We love only where it's safe to be seen.

But the soul knows better. The soul doesn't divide—it unites. The soul sees others as reflections, not threats.

In nearly every spiritual tradition, the call is the same: die to the false self so the true self can rise.

In Christianity, Paul wrote, "I have been crucified with Christ and I no longer live, but Christ lives in me." In Buddhism, the ego is regarded as the root of suffering—the illusion of a separate, unchanging self. The Tao Te Ching speaks of humility as strength and warns against the chaos of ego-led living. In the mystical teachings of Kabbalah, the ego is the shell that must be cracked to reveal divine light.

The mind divided cannot know peace.

Duality says it must be either-or. Spirit says: it can be both-and.

Yes, you were wounded—and you are healing. Yes, you've failed—and you are still called. Yes, you feel fear—and you are not that fear.

This is where healing begins: not by annihilating the ego, but by dis-identifying from it. By saying: I am not the voice that compares. I am not the fear that attacks. I am not the story that plays on repeat.

You are the awareness. You are the witness. You are the still space between thoughts.

The war in the mind will end the moment you stop taking sides and start observing. This is why meditation is not optional on the spiritual path. It's essential. Not because it makes you better—but because it reminds you who you were before the noise began.

Try this:

Sit still. Breathe deeply. When a thought comes, don't chase it. Don't judge it. Just see it. And let it pass.

This practice rewires your nervous system. It breaks the loop of reaction. It allows you to respond from peace instead of pain.

Because the truth is, the ego isn't evil—it's just afraid. Afraid of being forgotten. Afraid of being unimportant. Afraid of disappearing into the vastness of Spirit.

But you are not here to live small. You are not here to be driven by fear. You are here to remember the truth:

You are not your thoughts. You are not your wounds. You are the light behind the lens.

When the war in your mind quiets, the voice of peace returns. Not to shout—but to whisper:

"You were never alone."

Narrator's Reflection: The mind can be a noisy courtroom or a sacred temple. The difference is not the presence of thoughts, but your posture toward them. When we stop identifying with the ego's demands, we start tasting the freedom of the soul. Peace doesn't come from winning the argument—it comes from stepping out of the courtroom entirely. The ego always wants to be right. But the soul only wants to be free. Choose your witness stand carefully."?

6

STRESS AS A MESSENGER, NOT A MASTER

Stress wears many disguises. Sometimes it shows up as a pounding heart before a conversation. Sometimes it feels like a weight on the chest during sleepless nights. Other times, it becomes a low, constant hum in the background—a silent thief stealing joy, robbing rest, and making even the simplest tasks feel overwhelming.

For many, stress is a master. It dictates their pace, their decisions, even their identity. "I'm just a stressed person," they say, as if it were a permanent condition instead of a passing signal. But stress was never meant to be the ruler of your life. It was meant to be a *messenger*.

Stress exists because something within or around you is misaligned. It is not inherently bad. In fact, without the stress response, you wouldn't survive. The problem is not the presence of stress—it is our failure to listen, and our insistence on ignoring its message until the body begins to scream.

Imagine your check engine light flashing, and instead of fixing the issue, you just put tape over it. That is how most people deal with stress. They numb it, bury it, shame it. But stress, like pain, is a form of intelligence. A signal. A teacher.

The question isn't *how do I get rid of stress completely?* The question is *what is this stress trying to tell me?*

Is it telling you you're overcommitted? Is it revealing a boundary that needs to be set? Is it pointing to a relationship that is draining your spirit? Is it uncovering a fear you haven't faced?

Listen, and you will learn.

Spiritual teachings don't deny the presence of stress. They simply reposition it. They offer practices not to eliminate discomfort, but to transform it.

In the Psalms, David cries out, "When my heart is overwhelmed: lead me to the rock that is higher than I." He does not deny his stress—he redirects it.

In yoga, stress is seen as stored energy in the body—tight hips, tense shoulders, shallow breath. Through movement and breath, that energy is released.

In Buddhism, stress (or "dukkha") is a natural part of life, arising from attachment and resistance. By noticing without clinging or resisting, we find freedom.

The body speaks. The breath reveals. The soul knows.

When you ignore stress, it festers. When you fight stress, it fights back. But when you *listen* to stress, it becomes a friend.

Try this the next time you feel overwhelmed:

1. Pause. Don't push through. Take a moment to get still. Place your hand over your heart.
2. Breathe. Inhale for four seconds. Hold for four. Exhale for six. Repeat.
3. Inquire. Ask gently: What am I feeling? What triggered this? What needs attention?
4. Respond, don't react. Maybe you need to say no. Maybe you need to rest. Maybe you need a walk, a prayer, or a boundary. Act from clarity, not panic.

This is how stress becomes a messenger. It shows you what matters. It reminds you that you have limits. It nudges you to care for the vessel carrying your spirit.

Stress will always knock. You decide whether to let it guide you or govern you.

You do not need to live in a state of emergency. You do not need to earn your worth by exhaustion. You do not need to be everything to everyone.

Rest is holy. Boundaries are sacred. Your nervous system is not a battlefield.

Come back to yourself. Come back to your breath. Come back to the moment.

Let peace be your compass. Let gentleness be your path.

Because you are not behind. You are not broken. You are not too late.

You are a soul, learning to listen. You are a heart, learning to trust. You are a body, learning to heal.

And stress? It was never meant to break you. It was always meant to *wake you.*

Narrator's Reflection: We often treat stress like a flaw—something to hide, fix, or overcome. But what if stress is not the enemy, but a sacred invitation to slow down and listen? What if the tension is not punishment, but preparation for something greater? When we stop shaming our stress and start honoring the wisdom behind it, we shift from survival mode into soul-alignment. You are not here to live in reaction. You are here to live in response to the truth. Let stress speak—but don't let it lead.

7

THE ANATOMY OF ANXIETY

Anxiety is not just a feeling. It is an experience—visceral, consuming, and often misunderstood. To understand anxiety, we must first stop judging it. Anxiety is not a weakness. It is not a failure. It is the alarm system of a body that no longer feels safe, ringing even when there is no fire in sight.

It often arrives without invitation. You could be sipping tea, walking into a room, scrolling your phone, or sitting still in silence—and suddenly, your heart races, your stomach tightens, your chest constricts. A thousand thoughts come rushing in: *What if I mess up? What if they leave? What if I'm not enough? What if everything falls apart?*

Anxiety thrives in "what if." It cannot survive in "what is."

This is what makes presence so powerful.

To understand anxiety is to understand the body's survival wiring. The amygdala, your brain's fear center, is designed to protect you.

It doesn't care about logic or nuance—it cares about safety. And when it perceives a threat—real or imagined—it initiates the fight, flight, or freeze response.

The problem? Most modern threats aren't lions in the jungle. They are emails. Deadlines. Social pressure. Financial burdens. Childhood trauma that never got healed. Future outcomes we can't control. Unresolved grief we keep burying beneath performance.

So we live in a cycle: Perceived danger → trigger → body reacts → mind spirals → shame kicks in.

And the body begins to believe this is normal.

But anxiety is not your enemy. It's your alert system saying, *Hey—something isn't sitting right. Something inside needs attention.*

The challenge is that anxiety often gets tangled with shame. We start to identify with it: *I am an anxious person. I can't handle this. I'll always be this way.*

But you are not your anxiety. You are the one witnessing it.

Let's break down the layers:

1. Physical: racing heart, tension, shallow breath, fatigue
2. Mental: spiraling thoughts, catastrophizing, inability to focus
3. Emotional: dread, irritability, hypersensitivity
4. Spiritual: disconnection, lack of trust, inner silence drowned out

When all four are active, anxiety can feel like a tidal wave. So how do we return to shore?

Start with the body. When anxiety hits, trying to "think your way out" often makes it worse. The body needs safety first. Regulate before you ruminate.

- Breathe deep into the belly
- Splash cold water on your face
- Ground yourself by touching something real (wood, stone, earth)
- Move: stretch, walk, or even dance to shake off the nervous energy

Then tend to the mind. Use gentle, loving inquiry:

- Is this thought true?
- Is this fear based on the present or the past?
- What evidence do I have that I am safe?

Write your thoughts down. Speak them aloud. Interrupt the loop.

Next, feel the emotions. Don't shame them. Embrace them. Say: *I see you. I feel you. I will not abandon you.* Emotions want movement, not suppression. Tears are sacred. Shaking is released. Silence is a sanctuary.

Finally, return to Spirit. Anchor in truth. Return to prayer. Read sacred words. Meditate on your belongings.

In Isaiah 26:3, it says, "You will keep in perfect peace those whose minds are steadfast, because they trust in you."

Peace doesn't mean no anxiety ever visits. It means anxiety no longer controls the house.

Repeat this truth: "This is a feeling, not a fact." "This is a moment, not my identity." "I am safe now. I am loved now. I am held now."

Your nervous system can learn new patterns. Your mind can be renewed. Your body can unlearn the old responses. Your spirit can be re-centered.

You are not broken. You are awakening.

Narrator's Reflection: Anxiety often feels like a thief, robbing us of presence, clarity, and joy. But what if anxiety is not here to destroy you—but to direct you inward? To remind you to breathe, to check in, to come back to love? You are not alone in this. Countless souls have walked through anxious valleys and found light again. Let every tremble be an invitation—not to fear more, but to listen deeper. You are safe to heal.

8

WHEN THE SOUL FORGETS: DISCONNECTION FROM SOURCE

There is a kind of tiredness that rest doesn't fix. A silence inside that even music can't fill. A hunger that food, fame, or fortune can never satisfy.

That is the ache of disconnection. Not from the world. Not from others. But from the Source.

The Source has many names—God, Spirit, the Divine, Creator, the Infinite, the Light. But what matters most is not the label, but the link. Because when that link is strong, everything flows. And when it frays or breaks, even blessings feel burdensome.

The soul forgets slowly. It begins with distraction—when the external world becomes louder than the inner one. Then detachment—when we drift from our spiritual practices. Then doubt—when we question whether we're still loved or heard. And then despair—when we believe we're alone.

But here's the truth: You were never disconnected. You only stopped listening.

The soul cannot lose what it's made of. It can only be forgotten.

This forgetting is part of the human condition. Every spiritual tradition speaks of the journey away and the journey back. The Prodigal Son. The lost sheep. The wandering yogi. The desert prophet. The fasting mystic.

Disconnection is not failure—it's invitation. An invitation to return. To remember. To root again.

In today's fast world, disconnection has become an epidemic. Phones in every hand, opinions in every direction, content every second. And yet, never have so many felt so unseen. Never have so many felt so empty in a world so full.

Because content isn't connection. Noise isn't nourishment. Distraction isn't divine.

The soul thrives in stillness. The soul awakens in silence. The soul remembers in presence.

So how do we reconnect?

We begin with awareness. Ask yourself:

- When was the last time I felt deeply alive?
- When was the last time I cried from joy, not pain?
- When did I last feel God's nearness?

The answers may guide you.

Then, we choose stillness. Not to escape—but to listen.

Create sacred space. Light a candle. Close your eyes. Breathe. Whisper a name—any name—that helps you feel closer to Love. And wait.

No agenda. No checklist. Just willingness.

Sometimes the reconnection happens in a whisper. Sometimes in tears. Sometimes in laughter. Sometimes in the quiet sense that you are not alone.

And as the connection deepens, your energy shifts. Peace returns. Synchronicity reappears. Clarity unfolds.

You begin to remember: I am not alone. I am not my mistakes. I am not disconnected. I am known. I am loved. I am carried.

And that remembering is the beginning of healing.

Don't shame yourself for forgetting. That is the way of the journey. We forget so we can remember deeper. We fall so we can rise stronger. We wander so we can discover the sacredness of return.

Today is not too late. You have not drifted too far. Your soul still knows the way.

Close your eyes. Say it out loud: *"I remember now."*

The Source has never left. The connection is still alive. And so are you.

Narrator's Reflection: When the soul forgets, life feels heavy. But forgetting is not failure. It is a space of grace—a doorway to deeper remembering. God is not waiting with a finger of judgment, but with arms of welcome. Disconnection is a call, not a condemnation. And every time you return, the heavens rejoice. So breathe. Return. And let your soul remember the light it came from.

9

THE ILLUSION OF TIME AND THE BIRTH OF WORRY

Time is a teacher, but it is also a trickster. It structures our lives—past, present, future—but it is not as fixed as we think. Clocks measure it. Calendars organize it. But our souls were not born bound to it. In fact, many of our deepest fears are not rooted in the moment, but in the mind's perception of time.

We worry about what might happen tomorrow. We regret what we didn't do yesterday. We fear running out of time, wasting time, and being behind time.

But what if time itself isn't the problem? What if it's our relationship to time that births anxiety?

In many spiritual traditions, time is not seen as linear, but as cyclical or even illusory. In the East, teachings speak of the eternal "Now." In Christianity, God is described as "the Alpha and the Omega"—outside of time, yet present in all of it. Quantum physics now suggests time is far more complex than the ticking of a clock.

And yet here we are—chained to deadlines, obsessed with timelines, haunted by the past, and terrified of the future.

This is the birthplace of worry.

Worry does not exist in the present. It exists in projection. It imagines future pain, anticipates possible failure, and attempts to problem-solve tomorrow's problems with today's peace.

But peace is only ever found in the present.

The illusion is that control over time will bring peace. The truth is that surrender to presence will bring peace.

Let's break it down:

1. The Past is Memory. It is unchangeable. It is sacred, but it is not permanent. You are not what happened to you. You are not your old mistakes. You are not stuck in a story you outgrew.

2. The Future is Imagination. It has not arrived. You cannot suffer something that hasn't happened. Your brain may play the trailer—but the movie hasn't started. And you get to write the script.

3. The Present is Reality. It is all that is truly alive. Your breath is here. Your power is here. Your freedom is here.

So why is it so hard to stay here?

Because the ego hates uncertainty. And the present is the only space where certainty doesn't exist. There's no label. No story. No control. Just *being*.

The mind prefers to dwell on what it can explain, organize, or fix. But the soul? The soul is fluent in now.

Worry is a misuse of the imagination. Worry is a prayer for something you don't want. Worry is trying to parent the future when you haven't finished healing the present.

But what if we stopped? What if we brought ourselves back? What if we reminded ourselves: "Now is all I have. And in this now, I am okay."

The practice is presence. The goal is peace.

Try this:

- Sit for 5 minutes without an agenda.
- Notice the breath.
- Feel your body.
- Hear the sounds around you.
- Don't interpret. Just experience.

This reclaims the moment. This recenters your soul.

Jesus said in Matthew 6:27, "Can any one of you by worrying add a single hour to your life?" The wisdom is ancient and eternal: worry changes nothing—except your peace.

So what do we do with the past? We learn. We bless it. We let go.

What do we do with the future? We prepare. We trust. We surrender.

But what do we do with the present? We live it. We honor it. We embody it fully.

Every worry is a thief. But every breath is a bridge.

You are not late. You are not behind. You are not racing anyone.

You are here. And here is enough.

If time is a river, then presence is the raft. Stop swimming upstream. Let go of the calendar in your chest. Stop measuring your worth by productivity. Stop judging your value by how "on time" you feel.

You are timeless. You are divine. You are unfolding exactly as you should.

Breathe into that. Trust in that. Walk with that.

Narrator's Reflection: Time is a container, not a commandment. When we treat it as a ruler, we feel behind. When we treat it as a companion, we find flow. Worry only exists where presence has been abandoned. But presence—true presence—is a portal back to the sacred. Back to breath. Back to life. Don't waste another second trying to manage tomorrow. Come back to now. That's where peace lives. That's where healing begins. And that's where your power always was.

10

THE BREAKING POINT: WHEN THE MIND SURRENDERS

There comes a moment in every soul's journey when the mind can no longer carry the weight. When the questions outweigh the answers. When the mantras stop working. When the techniques feel dry. When the push to be "better" collapses beneath the sheer gravity of exhaustion.

This is the breaking point. Not the end. But the threshold.

The place where the ego finally says, "I don't know what else to do." And the soul whispers, "Good. Now let's begin."

Breaking is not failure. Breaking is access. It is the sacred undoing that precedes divine becoming. It is the moment the false self starts to crack so the true self can emerge.

But because we live in a culture that glorifies strength and productivity, we often fear this breaking. We label it burnout. We call it weakness. We avoid it with distraction, performance, medication, or noise.

Yet spiritually, the breaking point is often where grace breaks in.

Moses met God in the wilderness. Jesus faced temptation in the desert. The Buddha found awakening beneath a tree after years of striving. Mystics from every tradition speak of the "dark night of the soul"—a period of spiritual barrenness that becomes the gateway to transcendence.

To surrender is not to lose. To surrender is to be freed from the illusion that you were ever in control.

The mind is a powerful tool. But it was never meant to be your master. It is loud. It is proud. It is relentless. But it is not the source of your peace.

Peace comes when the mind bows to the heart. When intellect bows to intuition. When the will bows to wisdom.

Surrender doesn't mean you stop caring. It means you stop carrying what was never yours to hold.

There are things too big for your logic to solve. There are wounds too deep for your mind to mend. Only Spirit can reach those places. Only love can rebuild those ruins.

So what does it mean to surrender?

It means you stop trying to control what can't be controlled. It means you stop negotiating with your pain and begin to feel it. It means you stop praying for the storm to end and start trusting you'll survive it.

It means you fall to your knees, not in defeat, but in reverence. And you say: *"I don't know what's next. But I trust the One who does."*

And from that moment, something shifts. The tension loosens. The tears flow. The breath returns. And you realize: *I am still here.*

In that space, the divine can finally move. Not because you earned it. But because you allowed it.

Surrender is not a moment. It is a way of being. A continual release. A daily turning over. A minute-by-minute opening.

And every time you surrender, something greater fills the space you let go of:

Fear is replaced by faith. Control is replaced by trust. Chaos is replaced by stillness.

So if you feel like you're breaking, breathe. If the thoughts are too loud, breathe. If the pressure is crushing, breathe.

Then whisper: *"I surrender this. I surrender myself. I surrender now."*

Let your soul take over. Let grace do the heavy lifting.

Because some battles are not yours to win. Some burdens are not yours to bear. And some doors only open when your hands are empty.

Narrator's Reflection: The mind will fight to stay in charge, but there is a point where the heart knows what the head refuses to admit: we need help. Real help. Spiritual help. That's where surrender begins. Not in the polished prayer, but in the trembling confession. The true breakthrough doesn't come when you figure it all out—it comes when you finally let go. And in that letting go, peace rushes in like a tide. You were never meant to carry it all. Today, may you lay it down.

11

IT SHALL PASS: THE UNIVERSAL LAW OF IMPERMANENCE

Nothing lasts forever. Not the high, not the low. Not the joy, not the pain. Not the storm, not the sunshine.

This truth is both a balm and a blade. It cuts through attachment. It heals through perspective. It liberates by revealing that all things—no matter how heavy—are temporary.

This is the Law of Impermanence.

In Buddhism, this principle is called *anicca*—the recognition that all conditioned things arise and fall away. Everything is in motion. Change is the only constant. Even the self you think you are today is not the same self you were yesterday. Every breath is new. Every second, a fresh creation.

Why does this matter? Because most suffering stems from resistance to change.

We cling to what was. We fear what's next. We try to freeze what can't be frozen.

We want to hold onto love. We want to avoid grief. We want to stretch the good moments and skip the bad ones.

But peace begins the moment you accept: *this, too, shall pass.*

When you're in a dark place, that truth becomes light. When you're in a beautiful season, that truth becomes humility. Either way, it keeps you grounded in grace.

Impermanence doesn't mean detachment from life. It means a deeper appreciation of it. Because when you know something is temporary, you savor it. You stop taking it for granted. You stop wasting time holding grudges, nursing old wounds, or fearing change.

You start living fully, knowing the moment is precious.

And here's the paradox: Impermanence is what gives life its meaning. A flower is more beautiful because it fades. A kiss is more sacred because it ends. A life is more valuable because it's brief.

Spiritual maturity doesn't deny the waves. It learns to surf them.

You can sit in sorrow and say: *This won't last.* You can rest in joy and say: *Thank You for this while it's here.* You can meet endings with peace, not panic.

Because you know what others forget: Every death is a doorway.

The end of one thing is the beginning of another. The collapse is a clearing. The heartbreak is a holy invitation.

But how do we live this truth? How do we let impermanence guide us without becoming indifferent?

Start by observing the small.

- Watch a candle melt.
- Feel the wind shift.
- Notice how thoughts pass, how emotions rise and fall like tides.
- Reflect on your own seasons: childhood, old jobs, former friendships.

Everything that once felt permanent is now a memory. Everything you fear losing will one day evolve—or be reborn.

Next, release the myth of control. You can't stop time. You can't freeze people. You can't hold life still. But you can meet it with open hands.

You can say: *"I will love while it's here. I will grieve when it's gone. I will trust in the turning."*

Finally, embrace presence. The only moment you truly have is *now*. And when you bring your whole self to now, you touch eternity.

In Ecclesiastes, it says, "To everything there is a season, and a time to every purpose under heaven."

There is a time to laugh, and a time to cry. A time to hold, and a time to let go. A time to rise, and a time to rest.

Knowing this doesn't remove pain. But it transforms it. Because no feeling is final. No season is forever.

The ache you feel now will eventually lift. The confusion you sit in will eventually clear. The grief will soften. The joy will return.

Not because you forced it. But because that's how life flows.

The river moves. The stars shift. The tree lets go of its leaves and waits for spring.

So if you're in a moment of heaviness, say it aloud: "It shall pass." If you're in a moment of bliss, say it too: "This is a gift. It shall pass. Let me honor it."

Don't rush the season. Don't beg for permanence. Just stay awake. Stay grateful. Stay surrendered.

Narrator's Reflection: The mind craves security, but the soul dances in the unknown. The beauty of impermanence is not in making us fearful, but in making us faithful. Everything you're going through—whether mountain or valley—is moving. You are not stuck. You are not forgotten. You are simply passing through. So let go with grace. Hold with gratitude. And trust that nothing—absolutely nothing—lasts forever... except love.

12

FAITH AS FREQUENCY: WHAT YOU BELIEVE, YOU BECOME

Faith is more than belief. It is a vibration. It is a signal sent into the universe, into the spirit realm, into the cellular fabric of your being, declaring: *I trust what I cannot see.*

You don't have to see the wind to feel it. You don't have to see love to know when it's present. You don't have to see God to walk in faith.

Faith is not just a spiritual idea—it's a frequency you tune into. It colors your actions, fuels your decisions, and shifts your atmosphere.

In Hebrews 11:1, it is written: "Now faith is the substance of things hoped for, the evidence of things not seen."

Substance. Evidence. Faith isn't vague. It's tangible. Not to the eyes, but to the spirit.

What you believe shapes what you perceive. What you expect prepares your path. What you trust becomes the foundation of your life.

The question is not whether you have faith. The question is: Where is your faith placed?

We all believe in something. Some put faith in fear. Some put faith in failure. Some put faith in money, in people, in systems that were never meant to carry the weight of their soul.

But spiritual power begins when we consciously align our faith with truth, with love, with the Source.

Your faith is a frequency. And like a tuning fork, you attract what you resonate with. If you live in faith, you begin to draw in confirmation. Opportunities arise. Synchronicities appear. Doors open that logic can't explain.

This doesn't mean you won't struggle. But it does mean your struggle won't have the final say.

Faith is not denial of reality. Faith is deeper vision *through* reality.

It's saying: *"This may look like a loss, but I trust something greater is being built." "I don't know how this will work, but I trust that it will." "I feel fear, but I walk forward anyway."*

Faith is not loud. It is consistent. Faith is not flashy. It is steady. Faith doesn't always feel strong—but it always stands.

In every sacred tradition, faith is central.

In Christianity, Jesus said, "According to your faith, let it be done to you." In Islam, *iman* is the deep conviction of the heart, even without sight. In Buddhism, *shraddha* is faith that motivates practice and deepens experience. In metaphysical teachings, faith is an energetic alignment with your desired outcome.

Faith begins in the unseen. But it manifests in the scene.

You cannot claim peace and live in panic. You cannot declare healing and obsess over illness. You cannot ask for divine alignment and resist change.

Faith is trust in motion. Faith is alignment in action.

So how do we cultivate faith?

First, examine your inner language.

- Do your thoughts affirm possibility or predict doom?
- Are your words laced with trust or tainted with fear?
- Do you speak as someone who believes in divine timing—or as someone enslaved by worry?

Second, remember your evidence. Look back. Recall the times you were carried. The prayers that were answered in ways you didn't expect. The days you didn't think you'd make it—and yet, you're still here.

Write them down. Make them an altar. Faith feeds on remembrance.

Third, surround yourself with frequencies that match your vision. Music. Words. Community. Environments. Faith grows where it is watered. Starve the noise. Feed the knowing.

Fourth, act in alignment. Faith without works is dead. Make the call. Apply for the thing. Forgive the person. Write the page. Start the practice.

Every time you move as if it's already done, you align with the outcome you believe in.

You won't always feel it. Some days, faith will feel like walking through fog. But keep walking.

Faith is not feeling. Faith is direction.

Say to yourself: *"I believe even when I can't see." "I trust even when I feel unsure." "I know that what is for me cannot miss me."*

Let faith guide your posture. Let it shape your decisions. Let it hold you when doubt knocks.

Because what you believe, you become. Not overnight. Not always clearly. But consistently.

You are not here to merely survive. You are here to believe in more. To reach for what the world says is impossible. To walk in peace while others panic. To speak life where others sow fear.

This is the vibration of faith. Not blind optimism—but divine trust.

So tune your frequency. Dial into the eternal. And walk as if the ground is rising to meet your every step.

Because it is.

Narrator's Reflection: Faith isn't something you manufacture—it's something you remember. Something you return to. The quiet confidence that no matter how things appear, you are not forsaken. Not forgotten. You are guided. And the path ahead—no matter how unclear—is being made holy by your belief. Keep tuning in. What you believe is building the world you will soon see.

13

ECHOES OF THE BUDDHA: ATTACHMENT AND SUFFERING

More than 2,500 years ago, a man sat beneath a fig tree and vowed not to rise until he understood the nature of suffering. That man was Siddhartha Gautama—the Buddha. And what he discovered under that Bodhi tree still echoes through the halls of time.

His core teaching? *Life is suffering. And suffering has a cause: attachment.*

It sounds harsh at first. But the Buddha wasn't pessimistic—he was honest. And in his honesty, he uncovered the key to peace.

Attachment is not the same as love. Attachment is clinging. Needing. Controlling. Fearing loss.

We attach ourselves to outcomes, people, identities, expectations. We believe that *this thing, this person, this job, this version of life* will bring us joy—and if we lose it, we crumble.

But here's the spiritual twist: What you cling to owns you. What you can't release controls you.

The Buddha taught the Four Noble Truths:

1. Life involves suffering (*dukkha*).
2. The cause of suffering is attachment (*tanha*—craving).
3. There is a way to end suffering.
4. That way is the Eightfold Path: right view, right intention, right speech, right action, right livelihood, right effort, right mindfulness, right concentration.

The core of it all is detachment. Not detachment as apathy. But detachment is freedom.

Freedom to love without possession. Freedom to enjoy without addiction. Freedom to be present without demanding permanence.

Why is this so hard? Because the ego feeds on attachment. It finds identity in "mine." My success. My partner. My reputation. My image.

But what happens when any of those things change? What happens when the relationship ends, the job dissolves, the body ages, the applause fades?

The ego panics. The soul, however, smiles. Because the soul knows: *nothing external can define the eternal.*

Spiritual growth requires pruning. Sometimes the very things we're begging to keep are the things Spirit is trying to clear.

Detachment is the practice of holding loosely. Open hands. Soft expectations. Gratitude without gripping.

It doesn't mean we don't care. It means we don't collapse when things shift.

Imagine holding sand tightly in your fist. The tighter you squeeze, the more it slips through your fingers. But if you open your palm, the sand rests gently, unthreatened.

This is how peace works. This is how love works. This is how life flows.

Letting go is not giving up. Letting go is trusting there is more. Letting go is releasing the illusion that you are in control of every twist and turn.

The Buddha's wisdom was not meant for monks alone. It was meant for anyone who wants to be free.

Free from fear. Free from the tyranny of unmet expectations. Free from the lie that happiness lives in things, titles, or people.

Start small.

- Let go of needing people to understand you.
- Let go of timelines you've imposed on yourself.
- Let go of the story that you must always have it together.

Practice presence. When you eat, taste it fully. When you listen, be there fully. When you love, love without strings.

The Eightfold Path is not just about behavior—it's about alignment. Alignment with truth. Alignment with clarity. Alignment with what is.

You can love and release. You can strive and surrender. You can dream and detach.

Because the more you let go, the more room you create. Room for grace. Room for wisdom. Room for divine surprise.

Don't fear the fall. Trust the ground will rise to meet you. And if not the ground, then the arms of God.

You are not here to own. You are here to steward. You are not here to possess. You are here to pour.

Suffering isn't in the event. It's in the clinging. The fear. The resistance.

Peace comes when we align with reality. With the sacred law of impermanence. With the flow of Spirit.

So breathe. Relax your grip. Bless what was. Release what is fading. And open your arms to what's next.

Narrator's Reflection: The Buddha didn't offer escape. He offered awareness. He taught that freedom isn't found in running from life—but in facing it with open hands. Every attachment is a doorway to deeper understanding. What are you holding too tightly? What are you afraid to lose? In that place, peace is waiting—not in the clinging, but in the release. Let go, and know: what's meant for your soul cannot miss you.

14

CHRIST CONSCIOUSNESS: LOVE THAT TRANSCENDS UNDERSTANDING

There is a love that defies logic. A love that moves beyond religion, beyond theology, beyond fear-based morality. A love that heals without condition, that embraces without judgment, that walks into darkness just to bring back one lost soul.

This love is Christ Consciousness.

Not merely the man named Jesus. But the *mind* of Christ. The *heart* of Christ. The *frequency* of divine love that cannot be explained—only experienced.

In Philippians 2:5, Paul writes, "Let this mind be in you which was also in Christ Jesus." This is the invitation—not simply to worship Christ, but to *embody* His way of being.

Christ Consciousness is the radical love that sees the thief and calls him a friend. The adulterer calls her redeemed. The enemy calls them neighbors.

It's not soft. It's not passive. It's not naïve.

It is fierce, holy, and utterly free.

To walk in Christ Consciousness is to look at someone society has discarded and say, "You still belong." To look at your worst failure and hear, "You are still loved."

This love transcends understanding because it refuses to play by the rules of shame. It is not earned. It cannot be revoked. It doesn't wait until you've fixed yourself. It meets you exactly where you are and says, *"Come home."*

Jesus did not come to create religion. He came to reveal the relationship. To tear down barriers between God and man. To replace fear with intimacy.

When He said, "Love your enemies," He wasn't just offering a moral challenge—He was showing us how divine love operates. It's inclusive. It's expensive. It's alchemical.

It turns shame into testimony. Pain into purpose. Death into resurrection.

To walk in Christ Consciousness is to live from love, not for approval. It is to extend grace even when it's not reciprocated. It is to trust that healing flows through compassion, not condemnation.

But how do we embody this? How do flawed, fragile humans hold something so holy?

Start here:

1. See yourself through divine eyes. Christ never looked at people and saw only their sin. He saw their story. He saw their heart. He saw their *wholeness* beneath the wounds. You are not your worst

mistake. You are not your past. You are not what they did to you. You are the beloved.

2. Extend grace inward. The voice of Christ is not the voice of shame. It's the whisper of mercy. When you fall short, speak to yourself the way Christ would: with truth, yes—but with tenderness.

3. Practice radical empathy. Try to understand before you judge. Try to see where others are coming from. That doesn't mean excusing harm—but it does mean refusing to become hard-hearted.

4. Forgive. Deeply. Not to release them—but to release *you*. Forgiveness is the frequency of Christ. On the cross, His final words weren't of vengeance—they were: *"Father, forgive them."*

5. Serve. Christ Consciousness is not self-centered. It kneels. It washes feet. It feeds the hungry. It listens. It lifts. It loves without a spotlight.

6. Trust divine timing. Jesus never rushed. He moved in rhythm with Spirit. He knew when to wait, when to act, when to retreat, when to stand. Christ Consciousness is in tune with the eternal.

And when the world feels dark, remember: Light doesn't have to fight darkness. It just shines.

To carry Christ within you is not to walk in perfection. It is to walk in love.

To sit with the broken. To stand with the outcast. To forgive the unforgivable. To speak truth in the face of power. To carry crosses not for punishment—but for purpose.

Christ Consciousness lives in paradox: Strength through surrender. Victory through sacrifice. Wholeness through brokenness. Life through death.

This love cannot be mapped, but it can be mirrored. In how we speak. How we see. How we hold space for each other.

The Christ within you isn't asking for perfection. He's asking for presence. For openness. For willingness.

To say: *"Use me. Heal through me. Love through me."*

And in doing so, we become light bearers. We become bridges. We become living proof that love can win.

Narrator's Reflection: Christ Consciousness is not a theology to debate—it's a lens to see through. A way of being. A vibration that elevates the world by choosing love over fear, presence over judgment, healing over harm. You don't have to understand it fully to embody it deeply. You only have to begin. To open your heart. To love without keeping score. To forgive without a receipt. To walk like Christ—not perfectly, but faithfully. And in that walk, you become the sermon.

15

FROM THE QUR'AN: TRUSTING THE UNSEEN PLAN

There is a rhythm to the unseen. A pattern to the parts of life we do not understand. And within that mystery, there is something sacred: Trust.

Trust that what we cannot see is still real. Trust that what we cannot control is still held. Trust that what we do not know is still known by the One who shaped the stars.

In the Qur'an, faith is not merely belief in God—it is , complete reliance on Him.

"And whoever puts their trust in Allah, then He will suffice them." (Surah At-Talaq 65:3)

Tawakkul is the spiritual art of leaning—not on outcomes, but on the Creator of outcomes. It is walking into the storm and believing the ground will still appear beneath your feet.

Trust in the unseen is not a weakness. It is the greatest act of strength. Because it requires surrender. It requires letting go of your illusion of control. It requires placing your heart into hands you cannot see.

In a world driven by data, predictions, and proof, trust in the unseen feels like foolishness. But in the spiritual realm, it is currency. It is the quiet power behind every act of faith.

This trust says: *"I don't see the full plan, but I know there is one." "I don't understand the delay, but I know it is divine." "I don't know the why—but I know the Who."*

The Qur'an is filled with stories of people who waited, wandered, wept—and still trusted. Prophet Yusuf (Joseph), thrown in a well, imprisoned unjustly, forgotten by man but remembered by God. Prophet Musa (Moses), standing before the sea with Pharaoh behind him, trusting that the sea would split. Maryam (Mary), alone in childbirth, misunderstood, yet honored by the heavens.

Their stories are echoes of our own. They remind us: Your delay is not your denial. Your pain is not your punishment. Your confusion is not the absence of purpose.

The Qur'an declares: *"Indeed, with hardship comes ease."* (Surah Ash-Sharh 94:6) Not after. With.

This means even in the darkest moment, ease is already wrapped within it. You may not feel it yet, but it is present. Quiet. Hidden. Holy.

To trust the unseen plan is not to avoid grief. It is to walk with grief while knowing it's not the end.

It is to say: *"I cry, and I still believe." "I ache, and I still walk forward." "I do not know the way—but I trust the Guide."*

This trust transforms worry into worship. It turns anxiety into surrender. It turns fear into a deeper knowing.

It is not about pretending to be okay. It is about placing your heart in divine hands, saying: *"You see what I can't. You know what I don't. And you love me still."*

In this sacred posture, peace begins to rise. Not the peace of answers, but the peace of alignment. Not the peace of certainty, but the peace of closeness.

Because when you trust the unseen plan, you stop demanding signs and start looking for meaning. You stop fighting life and start flowing with it. You stop doubting your season and start honoring the seed.

The Prophet Muhammad (peace be upon him) once said: *"Wondrous is the affair of the believer. For there is good for them in every matter—and this is not the case for anyone except the believer. If they are happy, they thank Allah and there is good in it. If they suffer harm, they show patience and there is good in it."*

This is the path of trust. Not because it always makes sense. But because it always makes *faith*.

So how do we cultivate this kind of trust?

1. Return to prayer. Not just to speak, but to listen. To sit in presence. To pour out your heart, and then open your hands.

2. Reflect on divine names. In Islam, Allah has 99 beautiful names: *Ar-Rahman* (The Most Merciful), *Al-Hakeem* (The Most Wise), *Al-Wadud* (The Most Loving). When you trust these names, you stop trusting your fears.

3. Practice patience (*sabr*). Not passive waiting—but active trust. Patience isn't doing nothing. It's holding your ground with grace.

4. Seek knowledge and remember. Read sacred texts. Write your own story. Remember how far you've come. Reflection fuels trust.

5. Keep walking. Tawakkul doesn't mean you sit back and do nothing. It means you tie your camel, take the step, make the move—and leave the outcome to God.

This is divine partnership. You show up. God makes a way.

And when it doesn't look how you imagined? You lean in deeper. You say: *"Even this."*

Even this delay. Even this detour. Even this heartbreak.

"Even this is part of the plan."

Because the one who sees the unseen never loses sight of you.

Narrator's Reflection: To trust the unseen plan is to rest in the arms of something bigger than your understanding. It is to believe that life is unfolding exactly as it should, even when it's messy, unclear, or painful. The Qur'an invites us not just to obey, but to trust—to believe in divine wisdom, even when our hearts tremble. So today, whisper to your soul: *"You are safe. You are seen. You are still in the plan."* And keep walking. The road ahead is holy.

16

THE BHAGAVAD GITA'S CALL TO INNER BALANCE

In the sacred battlefield of Kurukshetra, a warrior named Arjuna stood frozen, overwhelmed by inner conflict. He was not afraid of swords or blood. He was afraid of what he might become. He was torn between duty and doubt, loyalty and love, purpose and paralysis.

And it was in this moment—on the edge of war—that Lord Krishna spoke. His words became the Bhagavad Gita. Not just a spiritual text. But a timeless manual for inner balance.

The Gita is not about war. It is about the war *within.* The war between what we want and what we know is right. Between comfort and calling. Between attachment and dharma.

Dharma, in Sanskrit, means sacred duty. The soul's path. Your divine alignment. And Krishna's call to Arjuna was simple and profound:

Act without attachment to the outcome.

Do your duty. Walk your path. But do not be enslaved by results.

This is the core teaching: Balance is born from detachment.

Not detachment from life. Detachment from ego. From the outcome. From obsessive control.

"Be steadfast in yoga," Krishna says, "and perform your duty without attachment to success or failure."

This is the paradox: You give your all—but you let go. You care deeply—but you don't cling. You move boldly—but you stay anchored.

Inner balance is not passive. It is fiercely centered. It is rooted in wisdom, yet responsive to life.

How many of us live in extremes? All or nothing. Burnout or avoidance. Clinging or withdrawing.

But the Gita teaches the middle path:

- Balance between effort and surrender
- Balance between intellect and intuition
- Balance between self-care and self-sacrifice

It invites us to ask:

- What is my role today?
- Can I do what is right without needing applause?
- Can I serve from fullness instead of fear?

Krishna does not promise ease. He promises *clarity*.

The moment Arjuna aligned with dharma—not ego, not emotion—his paralysis ended. He lifted his bow. He stepped forward.

And this is the invitation for us: To quiet the noise. To listen for what is *ours* to do. To walk in that truth, regardless of outcome.

So how do we live the Gita today?

1. Embrace sacred action. Do what must be done, even when it's uncomfortable. Feed the hungry. Speak the truth. Forgive. Show up. Do the thing your soul keeps nudging you toward.

2. Release attachment to results. You can't control how others receive your love, your work, or your honesty. That's not your dharma. Your dharma is to give fully and let go.

3. Cultivate steadiness. Meditate. Breathe. Pray. Journal. Anchor yourself daily so you are not thrown by every wave.

4. Recognize your triggers. Where you overreact, where you overextend, where you shrink. These are signs you're off-center. Pause. Realign.

5. Trust the rhythm. Krishna reminds Arjuna that this life is part of something eternal. What seems like chaos is often cosmic order. What feels like loss may be preparation.

Inner balance is remembering: You are not the storm. You are the sky. The storm comes and goes. But the sky remains.

This doesn't mean you become indifferent. It means you become *disciplined.* In your peace. In your power. In your presence.

The Gita doesn't ask you to be perfect. It asks you to be *present.* To live from the soul. Not the shadow.

Balance is found where the soul leads and the ego follows. Where your intention is clear and your attachment is light. Where you serve because it is who you are—not because of what you'll get.

Krishna says: *"A person is said to be elevated in yoga when, having renounced all desires, they neither act for results nor depend on actions."*

This is freedom. Not inaction. But *aligned* action.

Your life is not random. Your role is not an accident. Your timing is not off.

There is work only you can do. There is peace only you can bring. There is a path only you can walk.

And when you walk it in balance—detached from applause or approval—you become unstoppable. Not in the eyes of the world. But in the rhythm of Spirit.

Let this be your Gita moment. Let this be the day you stop waiting. Stop wavering. Stop questioning your worth.

Stand up. Lift your bow. And walk your path.

Not for the outcome. But for alignment.

Narrator's Reflection: The Bhagavad Gita is a whisper through time, reminding us that inner balance is not found in the absence of challenge—but in the presence of purpose. You are not called to control every result. You are called to act with love, release with trust, and stand in truth. When you do that, life moves with you, not against you. And your soul—the eternal witness—rests in sacred stillness, knowing: *I am enough. I am aligned. I am at peace.*

17

THE TAO OF FLOW: NON-RESISTANCE AND PEACE

There is a river running through all things. Not a literal river, but a current—a rhythm, a flow. It does not rush. It does not force. It moves with grace, patience, and quiet power.

This is Tao.

The Tao (pronounced "Dao") is an ancient Chinese word meaning "The Way." It is the eternal principle that underlies and unites all life. You cannot see it. You cannot grasp it. But when you live in harmony with it, peace becomes natural.

Lao Tzu, the legendary sage and author of the Tao Te Ching, taught that all suffering arises from resistance. Resistance to life as it is. Resistance to change. Resistance to truth.

"The soft overcomes the hard," he said. "Water wears away stone."

Non-resistance is not a weakness. It is wisdom. It is recognizing that fighting against what is only multiplies pain.

When we flow, we become like water: Flexible. Strong. Clear.

Water doesn't argue with the rock. It moves around it. It adapts. It stays in motion.

This is Tao.

And yet, we often live in the opposite way. We resist what's happening. We cling to how we think it should be. We tighten when life invites us to open.

Peace does not live in control. Peace lives in surrender.

Not passive giving up—but active alignment.

The Tao teaches: "Stop leaving and you will arrive. Stop searching and you will see. Stop running and you will find it."

Everything you chase is already within you. You don't need to conquer the world. You need to align with it.

Non-resistance means:

- Accepting people where they are.
- Accepting moments as they come.
- Accepting yourself as you unfold.

This doesn't mean becoming a doormat. It means choosing presence over panic. Clarity over chaos. Stillness over struggle.

It means saying: "This is happening. How can I move with it instead of against it?"

Try this: The next time something irritates you—traffic, delay, rejection—pause. Notice your body. Breathe. Ask: "Am I resisting life right now?" Then soften. Let go.

Feel the shift.

The Tao is in that shift.

Lao Tzu writes: "When I let go of what I am, I become what I might be."

Resistance keeps you stuck. Flow opens the door.

But we are conditioned to push. To control. To grip outcomes with clenched fists.

So how do we learn to flow?

1. Cultivate Stillness. When you sit in silence daily, you begin to recognize the inner river. You stop needing to force clarity. It rises on its own.

2. Release Judgment. Stop labeling every moment as good or bad. Start asking: What is this here to teach me?

3. Live Simply. Flow is obstructed by clutter—mental, emotional, physical. Simplify your space. Declutter your calendar. Say no with love.

4. Trust Timing. Everything has a season. You don't need to bloom out of pressure. Trust the unfolding.

5. Respond, Don't React. Reaction is resistance. Response is awareness. One creates karma. The other creates freedom.

In Taoism, the sage is not the one who controls, but the one who allows. Not the one who knows everything, but the one who trusts the rhythm.

You are not here to overpower life. You are here to move with it. To bend like the reed in the wind. To reflect like the moon on water. To let go like leaves in autumn.

Flow does not mean apathy. It means attunement.

When you flow, you begin to feel life differently. You breathe differently. You think more clearly. You love more fully.

You become a mirror of the Tao: Present. Peaceful. Unmoved by storms.

Not because storms don't come—but because you are no longer resisting the rain. You've become the river.

Narrator's Reflection: The Tao doesn't demand. It invites. It whispers to your soul: "Come back to flow. Come back to peace." When we stop fighting life, we start living it. And in that quiet, soft surrender, strength rises—not from striving, but from being. Let life move. Let love lead. Let the Tao carry you home.

18

THE SCIENCE OF STILLNESS: NEUROSCIENCE MEETS MEDITATION

Stillness is not a void. It is not emptiness or absence. It is presence in its purest form. A space where noise falls away, where breath returns to center, where the soul finds its rhythm again.

Science is beginning to confirm what sages, mystics, and monks have known for centuries: stillness heals. Stillness rewires the brain. Stillness brings the mind back to the moment.

Meditation, once seen as mystical or fringe, is now one of the most studied wellness practices in the world. And the results are consistent: Stillness changes everything.

When you meditate—whether seated in silence, walking in nature, chanting a prayer, or simply breathing with awareness—your brain responds.

Here's how:

1. The Prefrontal Cortex Activates. This is the part of your brain responsible for focus, decision-making, and emotional regulation. Meditation strengthens this area, improving clarity and reducing impulsive reactions.

2. The Amygdala Shrinks. This tiny almond-shaped cluster governs fear and stress responses. Long-term meditation reduces its activity and size, meaning less reactivity and more calm.

3. The Default Mode Network (DMN) Calms. The DMN is what activates when your mind wanders, worries, or ruminates. Meditation turns down this network, reducing anxiety and increasing present-moment awareness.

4. Cortisol Levels Drop. Cortisol is your body's primary stress hormone. Meditation consistently lowers it, leading to better sleep, digestion, and immune function.

5. Gray Matter Grows. Studies show meditators have increased gray matter density in areas related to learning, memory, and emotional regulation.

The takeaway? Stillness isn't idle. It's *active healing*.

Your body remembers trauma. Your mind collects clutter. Stillness is how you clear the static.

Stillness doesn't mean thoughts disappear. It means you stop being ruled by them. You stop chasing every idea. You become the observer, not the reactor.

Try this simple practice:

The 5-Minute Stillness Reset

1. Sit comfortably, eyes closed or gently open.
2. Place one hand on your chest, one on your belly.

3. Inhale for 4 seconds, hold for 4, exhale for 6.

4. Let thoughts come and go—like clouds passing.

5. If your mind wanders, gently return to the breath.

Do this daily. No pressure. No perfection. Just presence.

Over time, you'll begin to notice:

- Your reactions soften.
- Your sleep deepens.
- Your focus sharpens.
- Your spirit steadies.

Meditation is not an escape from reality. It is a return to *clarity*.

And it is not new. All spiritual traditions have offered stillness as a doorway to God.

In Christianity: "Be still and know that I am God." (Psalm 46:10) In Islam: *Dhikr*—remembrance through repetition and breath. In Buddhism: *Zazen*—just sitting, just being. In Hinduism: *Dhyana*—deep, uninterrupted meditation. In Judaism: *Hitbodedut*—spontaneous, personal dialogue with the Divine.

The external world is loud. But the soul is quiet. Stillness is how you hear it again.

In a world of constant motion, stillness is rebellion. But it is also a reunion. With peace. With wisdom. With your own sacred self.

You don't need a mountain. You don't need incense or a guru. You just need to *pause*.

To return to the breath. To return to the moment. To return to the knowing that you are held.

The nervous system thanks you. The mind releases its grip. The soul exudes light.

Because healing isn't always doing more. Sometimes healing is doing less—with more intention.

Narrator's Reflection: Stillness is not the absence of life—it is the fullness of it. In the pause, your body repairs, your spirit listens, and your peace resets. Neuroscience now echoes what ancient wisdom whispered all along: the mind heals in silence. The heart softens in stillness. And the soul remembers in quiet. So return daily. Even if just for a moment. Sit, breathe, listen. Your stillness is your sanctuary.

19

WHAT INDIGENOUS WISDOM TEACHES ABOUT TIME AND NATURE

Before clocks, before calendars, before digital noise and data—there was rhythm. The sun is rising. The moon is waning. The migration of birds. The rustle of wind through trees.

Indigenous cultures across the globe did not study time. They *lived* in it. Not as hours and deadlines, but as cycles. Not as something to beat or manage, but something to honor.

Time, to them, was sacred. It was not linear, it was circular. It moved like the seasons. It repeated with purpose.

And so did life.

Birth, growth, death, renewal. All mirrored in the natural world. And Indigenous wisdom taught that to fight these rhythms was to fight your own soul.

You are not separate from nature. You *are* nature.

The breath you breathe is recycled air from ancient trees. The water in your veins once moved through mountains and rivers. The calcium in your bones was born in stars.

Indigenous traditions remind us: We do not own the earth. We belong to it.

In the Lakota tradition, the phrase "Mitákuye Oyás'iŋ" means "All my relations." It's not just a greeting. It's a declaration of unity—with animals, plants, sky, water, ancestors.

This worldview doesn't divide the spiritual from the physical. It doesn't separate the sacred from the soil. It understands that the Spirit lives in all things. In the wind. In the rain. In fire. In silence.

What does this have to do with peace? Everything. Because most modern stress comes from disconnection. Disconnection from self. From source. From the land beneath our feet.

We forget the old rhythms. We forget to rise with the sun and rest with the moon. We forget to walk barefoot. To pray with our hands in the dirt. To see time as a teacher, not a tyrant.

Indigenous wisdom calls us back. Back to slowness. Back to listening. Back to reverence.

In Andean cosmology, the concept of *Ayni* means sacred reciprocity. Give to the earth, and the earth gives back. Live in balance with nature, and nature restores you.

In Aboriginal Australian teachings, the Dreamtime is not just mythology—it is memory, ceremony, and presence interwoven. The past is not behind. It walks with you. The land is not scenery. It is a living memory.

Time, in Indigenous eyes, is alive. It spirals. It teaches. It requires patience.

And nature? Nature is the original text. The first scripture. The sacred scroll with no ink.

So how do we reconnect?

1. Touch the earth. Take off your shoes. Feel the soil. Let your skin remember where it came from.

2. Listen to the wind. Nature speaks when we quiet down. Not with words—but with knowing.

3. Practice cycles. Honor your own seasons. Don't push summer energy in winter moments. Everything blooms in its time.

4. Give thanks. Gratitude was central in Indigenous living—not as performance, but as breath. Thank the land. Thanks for the food. Thank the water.

5. Live simply. The more you own, the more you must protect. Simplicity creates space for Spirit.

This is not nostalgia. This is remembrance. This is spiritual repair.

When you feel anxious—return to rhythm. When you feel lost—return to earth. When you feel overwhelmed—look to the sky.

The sun has never failed to rise. The trees have never rushed their growth. The moon has never been ashamed of her phases.

Why should you?

You are part of the circle. Not a machine. Not a mistake. But a moving miracle in a living world.

Narrator's Reflection: Indigenous wisdom doesn't ask us to conquer nature. It invites us to *become nature again.* To move with life instead of against it. To see time not as pressure—but as poetry. The earth remembers you. Let yourself remember it. Your peace is in the soil, the sky, the seasons. Let them guide you home.

20

GOD IN SILENCE: THE POWER OF LISTENING INWARD

There is a voice that doesn't shout. It isn't demanding. It doesn't argue or explain.

It waits. It whispers. It gently calls you back home.

This is the voice of God in silence.

In a world trained to fill every space with sound—podcasts, news alerts, playlists, conversations—we forget the sacred depth of quiet. But silence is not the absence of communication. It is the language of the soul.

When Elijah fled into the wilderness, broken and desperate, he encountered wind, earthquake, and fire. But God was not in those. Then came a still, small voice. A whisper. And in that whisper, the divine revealed itself.

Silence isn't empty. It's full of answers. But not always the kind you expect. Not quick fixes. Not external direction. But inner alignment. Soul-level knowing.

To hear it, you must pause. You must get still. Not to force a revelation, but to become receptive.

Because God doesn't force entry. God waits for an invitation.

And silence is the door.

Why is this so hard? Because we fear what we might hear—or not hear. We fill our lives with noise because silence confronts us with truth.

But if you can move through that fear, If you can sit long enough in the quiet, You'll begin to notice:

A peace beneath the panic. A presence behind the stillness. A knowing that says: *You are not alone.*

Spiritual traditions across the globe honor silence as sacred.

In Christianity: monastic silence as a way to hear the Holy Spirit. In Buddhism: noble silence to deepen mindfulness. In Sufism: silence as a doorway to union with the Beloved. In Judaism: the Hebrew word *"D'mamah"* means silence—but also, "thin silence" or "soft stillness" through which God speaks.

Even in science, studies show that silence regenerates brain cells, reduces stress, and increases mental clarity.

Silence heals. Because silence listens.

But it takes practice. It takes courage. It takes trust.

Try this:

- Sit for 10 minutes with no agenda.

- Let the thoughts come.
- Let the judgments rise.
- Don't follow them.
- Just notice.
- And breathe.

At first, it may feel uncomfortable. Boring. Loud. But keep showing up.

Over time, the noise begins to settle. And in that space, you'll begin to hear: The heartbeat of God. The truth of your spirit. The next right step—not shouted, but revealed.

Silence is not disconnection. It is deep communion.

It is the prayer beyond words. The worship beyond song. The clarity beyond striving.

And it is in that silence that peace makes its home.

You don't have to go to a mountaintop. You don't have to leave your life behind. You just have to pause. Turn inward. And listen.

Because the answers you seek are not outside you. They are buried beneath the noise. And silence is how you dig them out.

God has not gone quiet. You just need to be quiet enough to hear.

Narrator's Reflection: Silence is not a punishment. It is a sanctuary. In the stillness, you stop searching and start remembering. You realize that peace is not something you achieve—it's something you access. And in that quiet, you meet a voice that's always been with you. Not loud, but loyal. Not distant, but deeply near. God does not compete with noise. He waits in silence. Enter in.

21

THE BREATH OF LIFE: PRANAYAMA AND CENTERING THE SOUL

Before the word, there was breath. Before thought, before identity, before memory—there was breath.

It is the first gift we are given. The final thing we release. And the quiet rhythm that carries us through every moment in between.

Breath is sacred. In Sanskrit, it is called *prana*—the vital life force. The word *pranayama* combines *prana* (life energy) and (to extend or regulate). Thus, pranayama is the practice of consciously regulating breath to align body, mind, and spirit.

But this isn't just yogic poetry. It is science. It is healing. It is spiritual technology.

Because breath is the bridge. Between the seen and unseen. Between thought and presence. Between the flesh and the divine.

When your breath is shallow, you are anxious. When your breath is held, you are afraid. When your breath is steady, so is your spirit.

You cannot always control your circumstances. But you can always return to your breath.

In moments of chaos—breathe. In moments of heartbreak—breathe. In moments of awe—breathe.

This is not passivity. This is presence.

Pranayama teaches us that how we breathe is how we live.

Short, fast, and high in the chest? We live in reaction. Long, deep, and slow from the belly? We live with intention.

In the Upanishads, ancient Indian scriptures, it is written: *"Breath is the vehicle of the soul. He who breathes in, breathes in life."*

In Hebrew, the word for spirit—*ruach*—also means breath. In Greek, *pneuma* means spirit, wind, breath. In Arabic, *ruh* carries the same meaning.

Around the world, across traditions, the breath is sacred.

So how do we use it? How do we center our soul through the simplest, most accessible tool we have?

Here are a few foundational pranayama techniques:

1. Box Breathing (Sama Vritti)

- Inhale for 4 counts
- Hold for 4 counts
- Exhale for 4 counts
- Hold for 4 counts
- Repeat for 2–5 minutes

Used by yogis, Navy SEALs, and trauma therapists alike, this technique calms the nervous system and sharpens focus.

2. Alternate Nostril Breathing (Nadi Shodhana)

- Close the right nostril, inhale through the left
- Close the left nostril, exhale through the right
- Inhale through the right
- Close, exhale through the left

Repeat for 5–10 rounds. This balances the brain hemispheres and harmonizes masculine/feminine energies.

3. Ocean Breath (Ujjayi)

- Inhale deeply through the nose
- Exhale slowly while constricting the throat slightly

This creates a soft whispering sound, like ocean waves. Used in yoga, it creates internal heat and meditative focus.

4. Extended Exhale

- Inhale for 4
- Exhale for 6 or 8

This slows the heart rate, activates the parasympathetic nervous system (rest/digest mode), and brings deep calm.

You don't need a mat. You don't need a teacher. You only need awareness.

Breathe like your peace depends on it—because it does.

Breath is not just physical. It is energetic. It clears stagnant emotion. It moves old trauma. It returns you to the now.

Your breath is your anchor. Your reset. Your home.

So the next time you feel lost, scattered, or overwhelmed, stop. Place a hand over your heart. Place a hand on your belly. And breathe.

Inhale: *I receive*. Exhale: *I release*.

Inhale: *I am here*. Exhale: *I am enough*.

This is your portable sanctuary. Your inborn prayer. The life within your life.

Narrator's Reflection: The world may spin. The mind may race. But the breath remains. Always available. Always sacred. Pranayama is not about perfection—it's about returning. Returning to the body. Returning to the soul. Returning to the rhythm that was with you before words, and will carry you long after them. Let breath be your anchor, your teacher, your quiet liberation.

22

LOVE BEYOND EMOTION: AGAPE AS CONSCIOUS CHOICE

Love is often mistaken for a feeling—fleeting, conditional, and dependent on external behavior. But agape is different.

Agape is not a reaction. It is not romance. It is not an attraction. It is a decision. It is the highest form of love. Unshaken by mood. Unmoved by offense. Unattached to outcome.

Agape is love that *chooses*. It sees clearly—and still stays. It knows the flaws—and still gives. It recognizes the pain—and still believes.

This love is not sentimental. It is sacred.

In the New Testament, agape is the word used to describe God's love for humanity: *"God is love (agape), and he who abides in love abides in God."*

This is not a poetic metaphor. It is a spiritual reality. To live in agape is to live in God.

So how do we practice a love so high, so whole, so unconditional—especially in a world so wounded?

1. Agape sees without judgment. It recognizes the divine spark even in the darkness. It doesn't deny the pain, but it refuses to reduce people to their lowest moments.

2. Agape forgives preemptively. It lets go before the apology. It frees itself from the prison of resentment.

3. Agape gives without transaction. It doesn't keep score. It doesn't give to get. It gives because giving is its nature.

4. Agape stays aligned with truth. It doesn't tolerate abuse or pretend wrong is right. But it holds space for redemption. For transformation.

Agape is not weak. It is the strongest force on earth.

It is the power that turns enemies into friends. The power that restores broken hearts. The power that rebuilds what hate has torn down.

You've tasted it before. In the hug that asked for nothing. In the stranger who stayed. In the forgiveness you didn't earn.

And you've given it too. To children. To friends. To those who couldn't repay you.

Agape is your soul's native language. You were born fluent in it. But pain taught you another tongue: fear. And fear makes love feel dangerous.

But agape does not fear. It casts it out.

This is why agape must be a conscious choice. Not a reflex. Not a feeling. A decision. A devotion.

To love even when you don't feel like it. To bless even when you've been cursed. To hope even when the evidence says otherwise.

This is spiritual maturity. This is soul strength. This is peace in motion.

And the truth is, you are capable of it. Because you are made from it.

Every cell, every breath, every beat of your heart is held in divine agape.

So now it's your turn. To extend it. To embody it. To become it.

Not because it's easy. But because it's who you are.

Narrator's Reflection: Agape doesn't wait for perfection—it walks into imperfection with grace. It sees the worst and still chooses to love. This isn't emotion—it's eternity. The kind of love that forgives, endures, uplifts, and transforms. When you choose agape, you don't just love—you remember who you are. A vessel of the divine. A mirror of mercy. A keeper of peace that surpasses understanding.

23

MEDITATION BEYOND MIND: WATCHING WITHOUT JUDGING

Meditation is not escape. It's not a retreat from the world. It's a return to yourself.

Not the self made of stories or titles or pain. But the self that watches all of it with quiet love.

This is the heart of meditation beyond mind: watching without judging.

The world has taught us to evaluate everything. To label each moment as good or bad, success or failure, right or wrong. But peace does not live in labels. Peace lives in presence.

When you meditate—not to change but to witness—you begin to see how often your mind acts without your consent.

Thoughts rush in. Memories flash. Fears whisper. Plans dance.

And yet... You remain. Still. Silent. Watching.

This watcher is your true self. And it judges nothing.

It sees the sadness—and lets it be. It sees the anger—and allows it to pass. It sees the joy—and stays steady.

This doesn't mean you become passive. It means you become free.

Because only when we stop fighting our thoughts can we begin to understand them. And only when we stop judging our pain can we begin to heal it.

In Zen Buddhism, there is a phrase: *"Just sit."* Not to solve. Not to resist. But to allow.

This is radical in a culture of fixing. It's counterintuitive in a world obsessed with improvement.

But spiritual growth is not about force. It's about space.

Space to breathe. Space to notice. Space to let the mud settle so the water can clear.

Try this practice:

- Sit comfortably.
- Close your eyes.
- Bring your awareness to the breath.
- When a thought comes, say silently: *"That's okay."*
- Then gently return to the breath.

That's it.

You don't need to empty the mind. You need to stop identifying with it.

Because you are not your thoughts. You are the sky. And the thoughts are just clouds.

They come. They go. But you remain.

The more you watch, the more you awaken. And the more you awaken, the more peace becomes your default state—not something you chase, but something you *are*.

Meditation beyond the mind is not about control. It's about compassion.

And when you meet yourself with compassion, judgment dissolves. And in that space, the soul can finally breathe.

Narrator's Reflection: Watching without judging is the deepest form of love. It says: "You don't have to perform to be worthy." It reminds us that beneath all the noise, we are whole. Meditation is not a task—it's a return. A homecoming. Not to silence, but to self. Not to perfection, but to presence. You don't need to change your mind. Just learn to watch it—and let it pass like wind through trees.

24

THE GARDEN WITHIN: CULTIVATING JOY ON PURPOSE

Joy is not random. It is not reserved for the lucky. It is not something we wait for.

Joy is a practice. A planting. A garden we tend with intention.

Inside each of us is fertile ground. It's been trampled by fear, choked by weeds of comparison, parched by disappointment. But still—it's there. Waiting for seeds of joy to be sown.

The Psalmist said, *"Those who sow in tears will reap in joy."*

This doesn't mean joy comes after pain. It means joy can grow *through* it.

When we live reactively, we outsource joy. We tie it to outcomes. We hand it over to people's behavior, to numbers on screens, to praise or approval.

But joy that depends on circumstance is not joy. It's a bargain.

True joy—the kind that anchors the soul—is cultivated. It is chosen.

Like gratitude. Like forgiveness. Like love.

Joy doesn't deny pain. It lives beside it.

A mother in labor feels agony—and still weeps with joy. A mourner laughs through tears at a memory too sacred to forget.

Joy makes room. Joy knows the heart can hold it all.

So how do we cultivate it?

1. Begin with gratitude. Not for what you wish you had. For what you already do. Start small. Warm water. A kind word. A breath. Gratitude turns the ordinary into sacred.

2. Make space for beauty. Step into sunlight. Listen to music. Light a candle. Joy grows in beauty's presence.

3. Laugh intentionally. Watch a comedy. Call a funny friend. Tell a silly story. Laughter oxygenates the soul.

4. Give joy away. Send a note. Share your smile. Celebrate someone else's win. Joy given returns multiplied.

5. Create. Paint. Dance. Cook. Write. Build. Joy loves expression. Even imperfect. Especially imperfect.

6. Protect your peace. Limit drama. Mute the noise. Set boundaries. Joy suffocates in chaos. Give it air.

The garden within doesn't bloom overnight. Some seasons are slow. Some days feel fruitless.

But with each act of joy, you are watering the roots. You are telling your soul: I remember. I remember how to feel light. I remember how to hold hope.

Even here. Even now.

Joy is not the absence of sorrow. It is the refusal to let sorrow have the final word.

It is the wildflower pushing through concrete. The laughter in a hospital room. The sunrise after a sleepless night.

Joy is divine defiance. It says, "I will not wait to be happy. I will plant joy now."

Narrator's Reflection: Joy doesn't always arrive like lightning—it grows like a garden. Quietly. Steadily. Through seasons of rain and stillness. Cultivating joy is not naivety—it's resistance. It's faith with a smile. It's hope that dances. The world may give you reasons to be bitter. But your soul has roots in something deeper. Keep planting. Keep laughing. Keep blooming anyway.

25

AFFIRMATION: WORDS THAT REBUILD

Words can hurt. But they can also resurrect.

The words you speak—especially to yourself—are not harmless. They are building blocks or wrecking balls. They shape your identity, mold your moods, and inform your actions.

Affirmations are more than feel-good slogans. They are spiritual architecture. They are declarations that challenge inner lies and rebuild ruined places in the soul.

The Book of Proverbs says, *"Death and life are in the power of the tongue."*

And every spiritual tradition agrees: What you repeat becomes what you believe. What you believe becomes how you behave. How you behave becomes who you become.

So what are you saying? To yourself? About your worth? Your future? Your power?

So many of us are walking around with inner scripts written in shame: "I always mess up." "No one will ever love me." "I'm not enough."

These words don't come from the Spirit. They are echoes of fear, fragments of trauma, false prophecies we've agreed to.

But here's the good news: you can rewrite them. With intention. With truth. With words that heal.

Affirmations are not lies you try to believe. They are truths you are learning to remember.

Start here. Speak these aloud or silently—daily:

- I am safe to be who I am.
- I am worthy of love and healing.
- I am not my past. I am the lesson and the light.
- I am allowed to grow, to rest, and to begin again.
- I trust that everything meant for me is finding me now.
- I am enough. I have always been enough.

At first, these words may feel foreign. They might sit awkwardly in your mouth. But repetition rewires the mind. And in time, they start to sound like home.

Science supports this. Neuroplasticity—the brain's ability to rewire itself—means that affirmations can literally create new pathways. You're not just thinking better. You're building better.

Better peace. Better perception. Better possibilities.

This is why every prophet spoke. Why every mantra matters. Why silence must sometimes be filled with sound.

Because your words are not small. They are seeds. They are spells. They are bridges between who you were—and who you are becoming.

So bless your body. Speak life to your mind. Remind your spirit what's true.

"I am whole." "I am guided." "I am not what happened to me—I am what I choose to become."

Let your mouth become a sanctuary. Let your affirmations become prayers. Not because they change God—but because they change *you*.

They restore what the world tried to destroy. They rebuild what trauma tried to tear down. They resurrect what silence tried to bury.

Speak, beloved. Speak on purpose. Speak with love. Speak until the old words no longer fit. Speak until peace feels normal. Speak until the soul remembers its name.

Narrator's Reflection: Affirmations are not magic—they're medicine. A steady drip of truth that heals what shame fractured. With every word of life you speak, you take back power from the voices that once silenced you. So speak boldly. Speak gently. Speak daily. Because words shape worlds—and you deserve to live in one built on love.

26

FORGIVENESS AS FREQUENCY: THE VIBRATION THAT HEALS

Forgiveness is not a favor you grant to the unworthy. It is a frequency you rise into—for your own freedom.

You forgive, not because they deserve it. But because your soul does.

Bitterness is a prison. Resentment a parasite. And every grudge you carry has weight. Not on them—on *you*.

Forgiveness isn't a dismissal of harm. It is a refusal to carry it any further.

Spiritually speaking, everything is energy. And unforgiveness vibrates low—tight, constricted, heavy. But forgiveness? Forgiveness is expansive. Forgiveness is light.

It doesn't mean you forget. It doesn't mean you have an excuse. It means you release the hook. So you can rise.

Jesus said, *"Forgive them, for they know not what they do."* Not as weakness, but as wisdom. He knew the soul's peace depends on letting go.

And science agrees. Studies show that forgiveness reduces stress, lowers blood pressure, strengthens the immune system, and improves mental clarity.

But this is not just about wellness. It's about alignment.

When you hold onto pain, you stay linked to the moment it occurred. And that tether steals your energy from the now.

To forgive is to reclaim that energy. To say: "I will no longer relive the wound. I will rewrite the story."

This doesn't mean reconciliation. Sometimes boundaries are love. Sometimes silence is protection.

But the internal work of forgiveness is non-negotiable. Because where there's unforgiveness, there's spiritual congestion.

How to Begin the Frequency of Forgiveness:

1. Name the pain. Don't bypass the truth. Forgiveness starts with honesty.//
2. Feel it fully. Don't minimize it. The body remembers. Let it speak.
3. Separate the act from the soul. People hurt from their own hurt. Their behavior is not your identity.
4. Speak release. "I forgive you. I free you. I will free myself." Even if your voice trembles.
5. Bless the future. Pray for their healing. Not because it's easy—but because your heart is sacred ground.

Forgiveness is vibrational surgery. It clears the static. It reopens the channel to peace.

In Islam, one of the names of God is *Al-Ghaffar*—The Constant Forgiver. We mirror the divine when we forgive. We align with the infinite.

This is why every spiritual path includes it. Because you cannot ascend while holding anchors.

You deserve lightness. You deserve joy. You deserve peace not poisoned by past pain.

Let go. Not for them. For you.

Let forgiveness become your vibration. Let healing become your sound. Let peace become your default.

Narrator's Reflection: Forgiveness isn't an act. It's a frequency—a vibration your soul tunes into when it's ready to stop suffering. It's not about pretending it didn't hurt. It's about choosing not to let that hurt define you anymore. When you forgive, you don't just set someone else free—you set yourself free from the energy of pain. And in that freedom, the true healing begins.

27

GRACE IN EVERY SCAR: THE BEAUTY OF BECOMING

Scars don't lie. They speak of battles survived, of chapters closed, of pain that didn't win.

And if you look closely, you'll see: grace weaves through every one of them.

Grace is not the absence of struggle. It's the presence of God in the middle of it. It's the whisper that says, "Keep going." When your body is tired. When your spirit is cracked. When your hope is hanging on by a thread.

Grace is not always loud. It's not always pretty. Sometimes it looks like breath in brokenness. Or rest in resistance. Or light that won't go out.

You are not who you were. And that's the point.

Spiritual growth isn't about staying the same. It's about letting go of versions of you that were built for survival, not peace.

Those wounds? They changed you. But they didn't ruin you. They reshaped you. They deepened you.

You didn't just survive. You became.

Grace held you while life bent you. Grace carried you when no one saw you. Grace met you in silence, in stillness, in the sacred in-between.

In Christianity, Paul said, *"My grace is sufficient for you, for my power is made perfect in weakness."* That's the sacred exchange. Not power for perfection. But power through surrender.

In Buddhism, the lotus grows in the mud. In Hinduism, Shiva destroys to clear the path for new life. In indigenous wisdom, healing comes by honoring the wound, not hiding it.

Every scar you carry has holy fingerprints. Not because the pain was good. But because grace is greater.

You are not broken—you are becoming.

How to Honor Grace in Your Journey:

1. Name your scars. They are part of your story. Give them meaning.

2. Stop hiding the past. Your healing is proof that grace works. Let your testimony breathe.

3. Reflect with compassion. Look back not to judge, but to celebrate your survival.

4. Let gratitude anchor you. You made it here. There's beauty in that.

5. Share your becoming. Your story could be someone's spark. Let it be seen.

Grace doesn't demand that you be perfect. It invites you to be real.

To show up. To fall sometimes. To stand anyway. To let the light in through the cracks.

You are allowed to be a work in progress and a masterpiece at once. You are not behind. You are not too late. You are not damaged goods.

You are a living, breathing miracle of what grace can do.

Let your scars speak. Let them testify. Let them remind you: You didn't just survive. You grew wings.

Narrator's Reflection: There is grace in your grit. Beauty in your bruises. Power in your pain. Don't despise your scars—they're the signature of your becoming. Every one of them tells a story of grace that refused to let you quit. So wear them without shame. You are not what broke you. You are what rose from it.

28

DETACHMENT: OWNING NOTHING, ENJOYING EVERYTHING

What if the secret to peace was not found in possession, but in detachment?

Not detachment as indifference. Not apathy. But spiritual liberation.

To detach is to love without clinging. To enjoy without needing. To experience deeply without demanding control.

In the Bhagavad Gita, Krishna teaches Arjuna: *"You have the right to the work, but not to the fruit."*

This is the essence of detachment: Show up. Give your best. But don't chain your peace to the outcome.

In the Buddhist tradition, attachment is the root of suffering. Not because desire is evil, but because craving makes slaves of us.

To detach is to say: "I can be happy even if it doesn't go my way." "I can feel whole even when things change."

This is not a weakness. It's mastery.

The one who detaches doesn't stop loving. They love freedom.

They enjoy beauty without needing to possess it. They walk through abundance with open hands. They celebrate without hoarding.

This kind of soul is unstoppable. Because nothing can be taken from them that they have not already released.

Practices for Sacred Detachment:

1. Hold loosely. Each day, notice what you're grasping. Gently relax your grip.
2. Bless and release. Whether it's a relationship, a goal, or an identity—honor it, then set it free.
3. Anchor in what's eternal. Situations change. Status fades. The soul endures. Remember what lasts.
4. Celebrate without control. Joy doesn't require certainty. Let yourself dance anyway.
5. Trust the flow. Everything has its season. If it's leaving, trust it's making room.

Detachment is not about owning less. It's about being owned by less.

You can love your partner without clinging. You can enjoy your home without fearing its loss. You can pursue your dream without defining yourself by its success.

This is the way of freedom. This is the way of peace.

Detach, not to escape, but to engage more fully. Detach, not to avoid pain, but to live without chains. Detach, because joy is found not in possession—but in presence.

29

COMPASSION FOR THE SELF: THE FIRST STEP TO HEALING

If love is the root of healing, then compassion is the water. And you must begin by pouring it into yourself.

So many of us have been taught that kindness is for others. That mercy is for the weak. That self-criticism is noble.

But here's the truth: You cannot heal what you continue to shame.

Compassion is not indulgence. It is the only fertile ground where transformation grows.

The Dalai Lama once said, *"If you want others to be happy, practice compassion. If you want to be happy, practice compassion."*

And that includes you. Especially you.

Self-compassion does not say, "I'm perfect." It says, "I'm human—and that's holy."

What Self-Compassion Looks Like:

- Speaking to yourself like someone you love.
- Resting without guilt.
- Saying no when your body says stop.
- Releasing the need to be everything to everyone.
- Embracing your past without letting it define you.

Shame says: "You are broken." Compassion says: "You've been bruised—but you're still blooming."

In Christianity, Jesus extended forgiveness *before* people changed. In Islam, God is *Ar-Rahman*—the most merciful. In every tradition, the sacred is seen in softness.

So why be cruel to yourself? Why echo the voice of every critic, every abuser, every doubter?

You are not what they said. You are not what you failed at. You are not what you fear.

You are worthy of love. Even when you fall. Especially then.

Try this: Place your hand over your heart. Say aloud: "I am still learning. I am still growing. And I am worthy of kindness."

Repeat daily. Let it melt the inner ice. Let it rewrite the inner voice.

Healing begins when shame ends. And shame ends where compassion begins.

The journey is long. The road has twists. But you are still walking. And that is enough.

Let compassion be your companion. Let grace be your guide. Let your own heart be your healer.

Narrator's Reflection: Freedom doesn't come from grasping—it comes from releasing. Healing doesn't begin with criticism—it begins with compassion. In these truths, we learn how to live with open hands and soft hearts. In detachment, we move freely. In compassion, we rise gently. Peace is found in both.Chapter 1: The Cousins of Chaos: Fear, Doubt, Stress, and Uncertainty

30

THE POWER OF PRESENCE: RETURNING TO THE NOW

The past is a story. The future is a projection. The now is the only moment that's ever real.

Yet we live as if the opposite is true. Haunted by memory. Obsessed with what's next. Worried. Rushing. Distracted.

And peace? Peace is always found in the present.

To be present is not to ignore your past. It's to stop reliving it. It's to gather your scattered attention and offer it fully to the moment at hand.

Presence is not passive. It is the highest act of spiritual attention.

When Jesus said, *"Take no thought for tomorrow,"* He wasn't saying don't plan. He was saying: don't miss *this*. This breath. This heartbeat. This is sacred now.

The mind wants to roam. It thrives on anxiety, regret, projections. But the soul? The soul breathes in the now.

Presence is how you return to yourself. To your center. To the whisper of Spirit that can only be heard when the noise dims.

Practices to Cultivate Presence:

1. Breathe with awareness. Inhale slowly. Feel your lungs expand. Feel life entering you. Exhale with gratitude.
2. Engage your senses. What do you see, smell, hear, touch? Anchor yourself with what's real.
3. Set tech boundaries. Put the phone down. Let the silence speak.
4. Practice single-tasking. Do one thing fully. Not to finish fast—but to live slow.
5. Pause often. Throughout the day, stop and ask: "Where am I right now?" Then return. Return here. Return to now.

Eckhart Tolle teaches that all suffering stems from resistance to the present moment. When we accept the now fully—even when it's uncomfortable—we stop adding layers of pain.

Presence is the portal to peace. And it's always open.

In Buddhist mindfulness, awareness of the present is the path to enlightenment. In Sufism, God is met in the now. In every mystical path, presence is the gateway to divinity.

Because God is not in yesterday's shame or tomorrow's fear. God is here. Right now. In the inhale. In the stillness. In this very word.

Let presence heal your nervous system. Let it remind you that you are safe. Let it teach you that most of what you fear is just shadow—not substance.

When you return to now, you return to love. To clarity. To your truest self.

This is the power of presence: You don't have to fix the past. You don't have to control the future. You only need to *be here*. Now.

Narrator's Reflection: The present moment is where peace lives. It is where God speaks. It is where you are most free. So come home. Not to the past. Not to the what-if. But to this breath. This moment. This is holy now. In presence, you don't just find peace—you become it.

31

SACRED SPACE: CREATING AN INNER SANCTUARY

The world is loud. Fast. Demanding.

It pulls at your attention, your energy, your peace.

But within you lies a place the world cannot touch. A sacred space. A sanctuary. A quiet room in the soul where God still whispers and stillness reigns.

You don't have to go far to find it. You don't need a mountaintop. You don't need a monastery.

You only need intention. You only need breath. You only need to remember.

This inner sanctuary is not a fantasy. It is a spiritual necessity.

In every tradition, the idea of holy space is foundational:
- In Christianity, the body is the temple.
- In Buddhism, the mind is a garden to be tended.

- In Islam, prayer creates holy ground wherever it's practiced.
- In indigenous traditions, the earth and heart are equally sacred.

Your inner world can become holy ground. But it must be cared for. Cleansed. Guarded.

How to Create an Inner Sanctuary:

1. Choose a daily time to be still. Let it be sacred. A meeting with yourself and the Divine.

2. Design a physical space that mirrors your peace. It can be a corner, a room, a chair—simple, quiet, yours.

3. Clear mental clutter. Name your worries, then lay them down like coats at the door.

4. Set an intention before entering. "This time is holy. This space is healing. I am safe here."

5. Let silence be your companion. You don't have to fill it. Just sit with it. Let it speak.

The world may not change. But you will.

The storm outside may still rage. But within, there can be still waters.

The sacred space you create in your soul becomes your home base. When the day overwhelms you—return there. When anxiety spikes—return there. When fear rises—return there.

You don't have to escape life. You only have to create a room within it where Spirit can meet you.

Some call it meditation. Some call it devotion. Some call it a sanctuary.

Whatever you call it, make it real. Make it yours. Make it daily.

Because in that sacred space: You remember who you are. You reconnect with the Source. You rise from it with peace the world didn't give—and can't take away.

Narrator's Reflection: The soul needs stillness like the body needs sleep. Sacred space is not luxury—it's a lifeline. When you create that room within, you're not retreating from life. You're returning to yourself. Let your inner sanctuary become your strength. In stillness, God is not distant. God is already home—waiting for you to return.

32

THE ROLE OF RITUAL AND ROUTINE IN SPIRITUAL GROUNDING

In a world that constantly shifts, the soul craves something steady.

Ritual is not religion. Routine is not a restriction. They are anchors. They are bridges between the seen and unseen. They are the scaffolding that holds our spirit in place when storms come.

Rituals have existed in every culture since time began:

- The sun greeted with prayer.
- Meals blessed with intention.
- Candles lit for the ancestors.
- Feet washed before entering sacred space.

None of these rituals are about performance. They are about presence. They tell your body, "This is sacred time." They tell your mind, "We are shifting gears." They tell your spirit, "You are not alone."

Routine gets a bad name in modern life. We associate it with boredom, with being boxed in. But sacred routine is a form of freedom. It liberates your energy from chaos. It builds a rhythm where peace can flourish.

The Power of Morning Ritual:

How you start your day matters.

Do you begin with a screen or with silence? With chaos or with clarity?

Create a ritual that welcomes your soul into the day:

- Stretch in gratitude before your feet touch the floor.
- Light a candle and speak an intention: "Today, I walk in peace."
- Drink your water as a sacred act of renewal.
- Journal your dreams or affirm your truth.
- Breathe deep before the world makes demands.

You don't need an hour. You need presence.

Even five minutes of intentional stillness can shift your entire day.

The Beauty of Evening Routine:

How you end your day is just as vital.

Do you collapse in exhaustion or return to rest? Do you numb out or reconnect?

Sacred evening routine looks like:

- Washing the day off your body with mindfulness.
- Turning off electronics 30 minutes before sleep.
- Speaking gratitude aloud for what held you.
- Releasing what didn't go as planned: "It is done. I let it go."

- Reading words that uplift, not agitate.

These small acts signal the nervous system: You are safe now. You can rest. You are held.

Ritual as Remembrance:

We forget easily. That we're not alone. That we are loved. That we are more than our deadlines.

Ritual helps us remember. It invites Spirit into the ordinary. It turns brushing your teeth into cleansing. It turns lighting incense into calling on ancestors. It turns sipping tea into communion.

When done with awareness, routine becomes rhythm. And rhythm becomes a dance with the Divine.

Creating Your Own Sacred Rhythm:

1. Start small. Choose one part of your day to infuse with presence.

2. Name your intention. "This moment is for peace." "This space is for connection."

3. Repeat it daily. Consistency transforms action into meaning.

4. Protect it. Let nothing steal this time—not urgency, not guilt.

5. Let it evolve. Your spirit will change. Let your rituals grow with you.

Don't wait for a spiritual high to be grounded. Build your roots now. With simple, sacred routines.

Your rituals are not boxes—they are bridges. They take you from reaction to reflection. From scattered to centered. From empty to full.

And when life shakes you—as it will—you'll have something to hold. A pattern of peace. A muscle of memory. A rootedness that reminds you who you are.

Narrator's Reflection: The soul doesn't need extravagance. It needs consistency. Sacred routine is not about perfection—it's about presence. A small candle lit in the dark can anchor a whole night. A few whispered words can steady a storming heart. Let your rituals be reminders. Let your routines be a return. In their repetition, you will find your rhythm. And in that rhythm—you will find peace.

33

PEACE IN THE MIDDLE OF THE FIRE

Not after the storm. Not when everything is calm again. Not when the outcome looks favorable. But right in the middle of it—that's where peace proves its power.

There is a kind of peace that doesn't wait. It doesn't depend on resolution. It doesn't need all the facts.

This peace walks through fire and says, "Even here, I am held."

The great mystics, the prophets, the awakened ones—none of them were spared the fire. But they were sustained in it. Why? Because they found the place within where Spirit never flinches.

Daniel was in the lion's den. The three Hebrew boys stood inside the furnace. Jesus slept through the storm. Buddha faced Mara under the tree. Rumi danced through heartbreak and longing.

Each found that peace is not the absence of chaos. It is the presence of divine stillness *within* chaos.

Peace in the Fire Looks Like:

- Breathing instead of reacting.
- Choosing faith over fear.
- Speaking truth when silence would be easier.
- Staying grounded when everything wants to pull you apart.

The fire is not your enemy. It is your refinement. It burns away the illusion. It forces clarity. It demands surrender.

The fire says: Who are you without the comforts? Who are you when the image shatters? Who are you when the answers don't come?

And peace answers: "I am still loved. I am still anchored. I am still whole."

How to Cultivate Peace Mid-Fire:

1. Return to the breath. Let it remind you: You are here. You are alive. You are not alone.
2. Speak your truth aloud. "I don't know what's next, but I trust what holds me."
3. Visualize your center as unshakable. Let it be a flame that does not flicker—no matter the wind.
4. Remember your past deliverance. Recall the moments you didn't think you'd survive—but did.
5. Surrender the need to control. Let peace rise in the letting go.

This peace is not passive. It is not a weakness. It is fierce. It is holy. It is the voice that whispers in the flame: "You will not be consumed."

Because you are more than the fire. You are the one walking through it. And you are not alone.

Even here—especially here—Spirit walks with you. Not to put out the fire. But to make sure it doesn't take you.

Let the fire purify, not petrify. Let it teach you to find calm inside chaos. Let it introduce you to the version of yourself that only emerges when peace is chosen—not inherited.

Narrator's Reflection: True peace doesn't come after the war. It shows up in the trenches, sits with you in the furnace, and whispers, "You're not alone." Don't wait for the fire to go out. Find the stillness *within it.* That's where the miracle begins. That's where peace becomes power. for brevity...]

34

EMOTIONAL ALCHEMY: TURNING PAIN INTO POWER

Pain does not ask for permission. It arrives. Uninvited. Unannounced. It breaks. It burns. It bends.

But pain is not purposeless. And in the hands of awareness—it can be transformed.

This is the art of emotional alchemy: the sacred practice of turning emotional heaviness into spiritual gold.

Pain becomes power not when ignored, but when embraced. Not when denied, but when digested.

The mystics didn't run from their sorrow—they sat in it, prayed through it, transmuted it.

Rumi wrote, "The wound is the place where the light enters you." Jesus wept. The Psalms are full of grief. Buddha taught suffering as the beginning of awakening.

Pain is not a curse. It's a crucible.

The moment you stop resisting it and start listening, it becomes your teacher. It reveals your strength. It shows you what matters. It burns away the illusion of control.

How to Begin Emotional Alchemy:

1. Name the pain honestly. Let it rise. Don't sugarcoat it. "I feel betrayed." "I feel lost." "I feel unseen."
2. Feel it fully. Cry. Write. Scream if you must. Release without shame.
3. Ask the pain what it's teaching. What boundary needs to be drawn? What belief needs to be broken? What dream needs to be surrendered?
4. Transform the emotion.
   - Turn anger into clarity.
   - Turn grief into compassion.
   - Turn heartbreak into deeper love.
5. Create from it. Paint, sing, speak, write. Use the pain to build something beautiful.

You are the alchemist. The pain is raw material. The soul is the fire that refines it.

Pain may visit. But it doesn't own you.

Let your story be one where the wound was real—but so was the wisdom. Where the tears came—but so did the truth. Where you were broken—but not destroyed.

Because every emotion carries energy. And when you stop fearing it—you can direct it.

That's what makes pain powerful. Not that it disappears. But it transforms.

Like coal into diamonds. Like grief into grace. Like silence into song.

Your heart is a holy vessel. What it holds, it can transmute. And what once felt like death—can become the reason you live more fully.

Narrator's Reflection: Pain is not the end of the story. It's the forge. Emotional alchemy isn't about denying what hurts. It's about honoring it long enough to reveal what heals. When you hold your sorrow with sacred hands, it softens into strength. Let your pain speak—but don't let it steer. Turn it. Transform it. Let it teach you how to rise.

35

HEALING THE CHILD WITHIN

Inside every adult is a child. The child who once dreamt wildly. Who loved without hesitation. Who felt deeply and trusted fully.

But somewhere along the way, that child was wounded. Abandoned. Neglected. Told they weren't enough.

And though the body grew and the years passed, the child remained. Sitting quietly in your soul, holding the scars of yesterday, waiting to be seen, heard, loved.

Healing the child within is not about fixing the past. It's about restoring what was lost. It's about reclaiming the purity, joy, and trust that the world took from you.

The good news? That child is still there. Still worthy. Still alive in you.

But healing the child requires awareness. It requires the gentle, loving attention of an adult who can hold space for their pain.

This child is not a symbol of weakness. It is a symbol of hope. The child within knows things the adult self has forgotten. It knows how to laugh for no reason. It knows how to dream beyond limits. It knows how to forgive with ease.

And the first step to healing is listening. Not to the critic inside—but to the child.

How to Heal the Child Within:

1. Revisit your past with compassion. What wounds were never addressed? What dreams were abandoned? Sit with those memories without judgment.

2. Reparent yourself. Be the parent you need. Offer the love, validation, and nurturing that were once withheld. Speak to yourself the way you'd speak to a child: gently, patiently, and with infinite kindness.

3. Play again. Find the activities that once filled you with joy, and do them for no reason at all. Let yourself be free from "shoulds" and "have-tos."

4. Forgive the past. Not for their sake—but for yours. Release the people, the situations, the moments that caused harm. Make space for the child within to breathe again.

5. Speak affirmations to the child within. "I am worthy." "I am loved." "I am enough." Repeat these not just to your adult self—but to the child who still believes them deeply.

This is not regression. This is integration.

The child is not separate from you. It is you. But the adult you must hold the space for both—honoring the innocence of youth and the wisdom of experience.

When you heal the child, you heal yourself. When you give that child love, you give it to your whole being. And when you allow the child to dream again—you awaken the dreams of your soul.

Healing the child within is not a one-time fix. It's a lifelong journey. It's a return to innocence, not ignorance.

The child within never leaves you. It is not fragile—it is eternal.

And when you begin to listen, to love, to heal—it will show you a life filled with wonder again.

Narrator's Reflection: The child within is the key to your freedom. It is the part of you that still believes, still dreams, still trusts. When you listen to the child inside you, you reclaim joy, hope, and purpose. You are not broken—you are a healing, growing, ever-becoming soul. Embrace the child within, and the world will open its arms to you again.

36

THE PAST IS A PLACE OF REFERENCE, NOT RESIDENCE

The past is a teacher—not a prison.

It holds lessons, not life sentences. It holds roots, not walls.

But far too many live there. In that argument. In that heartbreak. In that moment someone failed to love them right.

They pitch tents in memories, replaying what went wrong, trying to fix what can no longer be touched. And in doing so—they miss the breath of now.

Why We Stay in the Past

The past offers something familiar. Even if it was painful, it's known.

And the known can feel safer than the unknown of tomorrow. We revisit past wounds hoping this time we'll change them.

This time, if we replay it enough, someone will finally say sorry. Or love us.

Or choose us.

But healing doesn't come from living in pain again.

It comes from walking through it—once—and letting it teach.

The Mind Loves Loops

The mind wants answers. It craves resolution.

So when something from the past feels unfinished, the mind loops:

- "Why did they leave?"
- "What could I have done?"
- "How did I not see it coming?"

But healing doesn't always come with answers.

Sometimes it comes with surrender.

You may never understand why they hurt you.

You may never get the apology.

You may never feel it was fair.

But you can still be free.

Because freedom isn't about erasing the past.

It's about no longer letting it own you.

Using the Past as a Reference

Let it be a map, not a cage.

The past can show you:

- What you will no longer tolerate.
- What patterns you need to break.
- What kind of love you truly deserve.

It can show you your growth:

- The ways you no longer people-please.
- The times you speak up instead of staying silent.
- The peace you now protect like treasure.

Look back only long enough to say: "I've come far."
Then keep walking.

Releasing the Residence

If you find yourself stuck in old rooms of memory, ask:

- What am I still waiting for?
- Whose validation do I still crave?
- What am I afraid will happen if I move on?

And then speak this truth to yourself:

"I cannot change the past, but I can change my relationship with it."
"I am allowed to be free, even if others stay stuck."
"I don't need closure to choose peace."

Practices to Let Go with Love

1. Bless and Release Letter:

    Write to the person or version of yourself you keep revisiting.

    Tell them what needs to be said.

    Then end with: "I bless you. I release you. I no longer carry this."

Burn it. Bury it. Let it go.

2. Timeline of Triumphs:

Instead of remembering only the pain, make a list of what you survived.

The choices you made.

The boundaries you drew.

The faith that carried you.

3. Create a Ritual of Closure:

   Light a candle. Say a prayer.

   Create a symbolic gesture that marks the end of your emotional tenancy in the past.

   It may not erase it—but it honors your decision to move forward.

4. Anchor in the Present:

   Name five things you can touch.

   Four things you can see.

   Three things you can hear.

   Two things you can smell.

   One thing you can feel inside: peace, even if small.

   You're here. You're safe. You're not back there anymore.

Grace for the Journey

Healing is not linear.

You may think you've left the past only to revisit it unexpectedly. That's okay.

But now you know not to unpack your bags.

Not to redecorate the pain.

Not to let shame convince you that you haven't grown.

Just visit. Observe. And come back home—to the present.

You Are Not Your Story

You may have been broken.
But you are not broken.

You may have been abandoned.
But you are not abandoned.

You may have experienced trauma.
But you are not trauma.

Your story shaped you—but it doesn't define you.

You are the author now.
And you get to write the next chapter.

What Freedom Feels Like

- Waking up without resentment.
- Hearing their name without flinching.
- Loving again without fear.
- Looking back without getting stuck.

Peace doesn't mean forgetting.
It means remembering with gentleness.

The scar may remain.

But the wound no longer bleeds.

Affirm This Daily:

"I remember, but I don't relive."

"I honor the past, but I don't belong to it."

"I choose presence over pain."

Because the truth is:

You can't change what was.

But you can choose who you become.

And you are not bound to yesterday.

You are free to build today.

Narrator's Reflection:

The past is sacred—but it is not sovereign. It cannot hold your future hostage unless you give it the keys. Bless what it taught you. Mourn what it cost you. Then walk forward. Because real peace isn't found in the past—it's claimed in the present.

37

BREAKING GENERATIONAL CURSES THROUGH CONSCIOUS LIVING

We inherit more than eye color, blood type, or last names.

We inherit patterns.

Patterns of silence.

Patterns of survival.

Patterns of pain dressed up as tradition.

Some call it "just the way it is."

But what it really is—are unhealed wounds passed from hand to hand, heart to heart.

Generational curses are not just mystical phrases or Sunday sermons.
They are behavioral scripts rehearsed in families until someone forgets they can be rewritten.

- A father never says "I love you."
- A mother uses shame as discipline.
- A family avoids hard conversations.
- Abuse is explained away.
- Secrets sit at the dinner table like guests.

And no one dares question it—until someone does.

That someone… might be you.

What Is a Generational Curse, Really?

It's a cycle.

A loop that repeats until consciousness interrupts it.

It's inherited trauma.

Conditioned behavior.

Pain that was normalized—and never processed.

You may have been taught:

- Money is evil.
- Love must be earned.
- Rest is laziness.
- Emotions are weak.
- Anger is strength.

But that doesn't make it true.

It just makes it familiar.

And familiarity isn't always safety—it's just repetition.

The Power of Awareness

The moment you become aware, the curse begins to crack.

Conscious living is the practice of *noticing*.

Noticing what's automatic.

Noticing what doesn't feel aligned.

Noticing what you do just because it was done to you.

To live consciously means asking:

- Why do I believe this?
- Where did I learn this?
- Is this truth or trauma?
- Is this love or fear in disguise?

When you stop living by default—you start living by design.

You Don't Have to Repeat the Script

They may have stayed silent.
But you speak.

They may have numbed themselves with addiction.
But you choose healing.

They may have been punished instead of parenting.
But you love with presence and patience.

They may have hidden.
But you bring things to light.

Conscious Living Looks Like:

- Apologizing to your children when you're wrong.
- Pausing before reacting.
- Reading books your parents never read.
- Going to therapy instead of pretending.

- Teaching your family to pray, breathe, journal, forgive.
- Not repeating what once felt normal—but never felt right.

You are not betraying your family by changing.

You are blessing them with freedom they never had.

What Makes It So Hard

Healing isn't just hard—it's heavy.

Because you're not just facing your wounds.

You're holding what others refused to.

You're grieving for what happened to you.

But also for what happened to them.

You begin to see your parents not as villains—but as wounded children who never got to heal.

And suddenly, you find yourself crying for them.

And for the child in you who had to grow up too soon.

But that's what breaks the curse: empathy without enmeshment.

You love them, but you don't mimic them.

You see them, but you don't surrender to their blindness.

You forgive them, but you don't forget yourself.

You Don't Have to Be Perfect to Break the Pattern

You just have to be *present*.

You just have to *see it*.

You don't have to raise perfect kids.

You just have to raise them without the lies you were told.

You don't have to have it all figured out.

You just have to be willing to do it differently.

Even a 1% shift in you becomes a 100% change in the generation that follows.

Tools for Conscious Breakers

1. Speak What Was Once Silent
2. Have the conversations that were avoided.
3. Name the trauma. Acknowledge the pain.
4. Let it breathe in the open air where it can't grow in the dark.
5. Daily Self-Awareness Check-Ins
6. Ask yourself: "Am I reacting from the wound or the healed part of me?"

    This one question can pause a thousand patterns.

    Create Rituals That Renew

    Light a candle before meals.

    Pray together.

    Share highs and lows each evening.

    Make emotional check-ins part of your family culture.

7. Honor Your Body's Intelligence

Your nervous system often knows before your mind catches up.
Notice tension. Notice shutdown.
These are signals that you're touching a generational edge—and it's time to breathe and choose differently.

8. Write a New Family Manifesto

What do you stand for now?
What values will you embody?
What language will be normal in your home?
Make it visible. Make it real.

A new legacy starts with a new language.

Affirmations for Generational Breakers

"I am the one my bloodline prayed for."

"I forgive without forgetting who I am."

"I break patterns, not people." "I hold the past with compassion and the future with strength."

"It ends with me—and begins with me."

Let Grace Lead

You will make mistakes.

You will forget.

You will slip.

That's okay.

Breaking curses isn't about being flawless.

It's about being faithful to the journey.

One honest apology can undo generations of shame.

One boundary can end decades of dysfunction.

One deep breath can silence a thousand echoes.

Your Children Will Thank You

Not always with words.

But with their peace.

With their joy.

With their freedom to feel and be and become.

And your ancestors?

Even if they never said it in life—on some soul level, they know.

They see.

They bless your bravery.

Because what you do now doesn't just heal downward—it heals backward too.

You Are the Bridge

Between what was and what will never be again.

Between dysfunction and clarity.

Between silence and truth.

Between wounds and wisdom.

And when you look back years from now, you'll smile and say:

"I didn't know how to do it all—but I knew how to start."

And that… was enough.

Narrator's Reflection:

To break a curse is to love with eyes wide open. To see what was, bless what you can, and walk forward with sacred defiance. Conscious living is the loudest "no more" you can offer to the pain that never belonged to you in the first place. You are not just healing—you are re-writing destiny.

38

VIBRATION AND HEALING: ENERGY WORK AND FREQUENCY

Everything is energy.

Not just the lights in your home, or the waves in the ocean.

You.

Your thoughts.

Your emotions.

Your words.

All vibrating.

All creating frequencies that either heal or harm.

The truth is, your body isn't just flesh and bone.

It's sound.

It's light.

It's rhythm.

It's a living symphony of frequencies—each cell humming a note, each thought tuning that note higher or lower.

Why Vibration Matters

When ancient texts spoke of "the Word" creating the universe, they weren't being poetic.
They were pointing to the truth that vibration—sound—*is* creation.

Everything you say, think, or believe carries a frequency.
And that frequency either aligns you with health, clarity, and peace—or pulls you into chaos, illness, and heaviness.

Low vibrations feel like:

- Chronic fear.
- Anger without outlet.
- Despair that sits in the bones.
- Judgment, guilt, shame.

High vibrations feel like:

- Love.
- Gratitude.
- Joy.
- Forgiveness.
- Stillness.

The question is not whether you vibrate.

The question is: *at what frequency are you living your life?*

You Don't Need to Be a Guru

You don't need to chant on a mountain or burn sage in every room to understand energy.

Every time you walk into a space and "feel tension," that's energy.

Every time someone texts you and you instantly get anxious or warm inside, that's a vibration.

Every time a song lifts you or a voice drains you, it's frequency meeting your nervous system.

Your body speaks energy fluently.

The question is whether you're listening.

The Science Meets the Spirit

Quantum physics confirms it.

Everything at its core is vibration—particles in motion.

Your heart has an electromagnetic field that can be felt up to 10 feet away.

Your emotions release hormones that change the chemistry of every organ.

And even your thoughts—those silent whispers—carry measurable energy.

This isn't spiritual fluff.

It's a spiritual fact.

Healing Through Frequency

Have you ever noticed how a single sound can bring you to tears?

Or how certain environments calm your anxiety without explanation?

That's not just memory.
It's energy alignment.

Different healing modalities work by restoring balance to your vibrational field.

Some examples include:

1. Sound Healing – using singing bowls, tuning forks, chimes, or mantras to realign dissonant frequencies in the body.

2. Reiki & Energy Healing – transmitting high-vibrational life force energy into places blocked by emotional or physical pain.

3. Breathwork – altering your breath to shift your energetic state. Shallow breath = survival mode. Deep, slow breath = peace.

4. Chakra Balancing – the ancient system of seven energy centers in the body, each associated with specific emotions, colors, and organs.

5. Color Therapy – using specific colors to stimulate or soothe different emotional and physical centers.

6. Music & Nature – immersing yourself in soundscapes and frequencies that naturally harmonize your nervous system.

Healing doesn't always come in words.

Sometimes it comes in tones, in colors, in silence.

Raising Your Vibration Daily

You don't need candles or crystals to begin.

Energy is everywhere.

You just need awareness.

Start with these practices:

1. Speak with Intention.

    Words carry frequency. Saying "I can't" vibrates differently than "I'm learning."

    Speak to yourself the way love would.

2. Protect Your Field.
    Not everyone is allowed to dump their chaos into your space.
    Boundaries are energetic filters. Use them without guilt.

3. Eat Light, Think Light.

    Food is frequency.

    Plants hold more light. Processed foods dull your field.

    What you digest affects how you vibrate.

4. Breathe Like It Matters.

    Inhale 4. Hold 4. Exhale 8.

    This slows your frequency and clears static in the body.

5. Forgive Quickly.

    Bitterness is one of the lowest vibrations on Earth.

    Release it—not for them, but for your healing.

6. Meditate in Stillness.
    Stillness is the tuning fork for the soul.
    Silence realigns you to divine resonance.

7. Music as Medicine.
    Curate playlists that lift your spirit.
    Let frequency do what words sometimes can't.

People Are Frequencies Too

Not everyone deserves access to your vibration.

Be mindful:

- Who drains you?
- Who inspires you?
- Who matches your peace, not your wounds?

You become like the energy you stay around.
Choose wisely.

What Happens When You Raise Your Frequency

- Opportunities begin to flow with less resistance.
- You attract people who see your worth instead of your wounds.
- Your body begins to heal itself—because it's no longer under constant energetic attack.
- You stop chasing and start attracting.
- Peace becomes your default, not your reward.

Affirm This Daily

"I am energy in motion."
"My vibration creates my experience."
"I release what lowers me. I rise with intention."
"I am in harmony with what heals me."

The Planet Feels It Too

When enough individuals raise their vibration, it affects the collective field.

Wars end when enough hearts beat with peace.
Systems crumble when truth vibrates louder than fear.
New worlds form when souls begin to remember who they are.

You are not just healing you.
You're healing timelines.

Sacred Truth

God is vibration.

Love is the highest frequency.

And every step you take toward peace—every breath of gratitude, every moment of forgiveness—is a return to that divine rhythm.

You don't have to shout to be powerful.
Your stillness can shake the earth.

Your healing hum becomes a harmony others can follow.
That's how worlds change.

Narrator's Reflection
It does not matter trying to become spiritual. You are a spirit, vibrating in temporary form. When you understand this, healing becomes a tuning, not a striving. Choose your frequency like your life depends on it—because it does. You are a vibration. A healing. A living, breathing sound of God remembering itself.

39

THE ROLE OF NATURE IN SPIRITUAL RECONNECTION

Before there were churches, temples, or sacred texts—
There were trees.
There were stars.
 here was wind that spoke to the soul and water that knew how to cleanse more than just skin.

Nature was the first sanctuary.
And still is.

Long before you understood the language of doctrine, you felt the stillness of morning dew, the crackle of fire, the heartbeat of the earth beneath bare feet.

In that silence, you weren't confused about who you were.
You were whole.

But in a world of cement and screens, schedules and sirens, that connection has faded—not because nature stopped speaking, but because we stopped listening.

And yet, it waits.
Patient.
Alive.
Ready to heal us again.

We Belong to the Earth, Not the Other Way Around

Our modern minds have flipped the order.
We speak of "owning" land, "controlling" nature, "mastering" the environment.

But the soul knows better.

We don't own the land.
We are born of it.

- Your breath is made of trees.
- Your bones are forged from minerals deep in the soil.
- Your blood mirrors the ocean's salt.
- Your heart pulses with the rhythm of the tides.

You don't visit nature—you *are* nature.

You are not separate. You are a living, breathing extension of the planet's spirit.

Why Nature Heals So Deeply

Because it doesn't judge.

It doesn't care what degree you hold, what mistakes you've made, or how long you've been running from yourself.

It simply offers its presence.

The sun warms all equally.
The river does not ask if you're worthy before it quenches your thirst.
The moon rises even for those who feel undeserving of light.

Nature teaches unconditional acceptance—without ever using words.

And when you sit in it, you remember how to accept yourself.

Natural Elements That Reconnect You

1. Earth – Grounding
   When you walk barefoot on soil or grass, you literally reconnect your body's electromagnetic field with the earth's.
   This isn't symbolic—it's science.
   Grounding has been shown to reduce inflammation, lower cortisol (stress hormone), and balance nervous system activity.

But more than that—it reminds you:
You are supported.

2. Water – Cleansing
   Oceans, lakes, showers, tears.
   Water holds emotion.
   It teaches flow, forgiveness, and surrender.

When you sit by water, you don't need to understand your pain—you just need to let it move through you.

Water never resists the shape it's poured into.
And yet, it carves canyons.

That's what surrender looks like.

3. Air – Clarity
   A deep breath in the forest carries more than oxygen.
   It carries life force—prana, chi, spirit.

When you breathe in fresh air, you invite presence.
You slow down.
You return to now.

4. Fire – Transformation
   The flicker of a flame. The heat of the sun.
   Fire teaches transmutation.

What looks like destruction is often rebirth.
Ashes aren't ends—they are the soil of something new.

When you light a candle with intention, you signal to the universe: "I'm ready to be changed."

5. Space – Stillness
   The space between trees. The silence between waves.
   Nature doesn't rush.

It grows in rhythm.
It waits in wisdom.
It doesn't force a bloom.

It reminds you: You are not late. You are becoming.

Daily Ways to Reconnect with Nature

1. Step Outside—Barefoot if You Can
   Feel the dirt, the cold, the life beneath your feet. Let it recalibrate your nervous system.

2. Watch the Sky
   Sunrises, sunsets, stars.
   They realign your sense of time—and remind you of the vastness holding you.

3. Grow Something
   Even a small plant in your window teaches you patience, nourishment, and responsibility.

4. Drink Water with Reverence
   Bless your water. Speak love into it before you sip.
   Water carries memory—and responds to intention.

5. Walk Without a Destination
   Let nature set the pace. Let your spirit wander.
   Answers often come when questions are quiet.

6. Use Nature in Your Rituals
   Burn herbs. Create altar spaces with stones, feathers, wood.
   Not as decoration—but as co-participants in your healing.

Nature And The Nervous System

Scientific studies now confirm what sages have known for centuries:

- 20 minutes in nature reduces cortisol and blood pressure.
- Forest bathing (Shinrin-yoku) improves mood, immunity, and sleep.
- Listening to natural sounds like rainfall, birdsong, and wind boosts focus and emotional regulation.

But beyond the studies, you already know this.

You know how your breath slows when you're near the ocean.
How your heart softens under starlight.
How your thoughts are quiet in the woods.

That's your body remembering what your mind forgets:
You were made for this connection.

Sacred Practices to Deepen Your Bond

- Full Moon Release:
  Write down what you're letting go. Burn the paper under

the moon.
Let the sky witness your surrender.
- New Moon Intentions:
  Plant seeds—literally or symbolically. Bury dreams in the soil. Let Earth partner in their birth.
- Wind Walks:
  Go out when the wind is strong. Let it carry away stagnant energy.
  Imagine it brushing old pain off your skin.
- Nature Journaling:
  Sit under a tree. Observe without needing to analyze.
  Write what you see. What you feel. What you remember.

The More You Return to Nature, the More You Return to You

You begin to:

- Breathe deeper.
- Speak gentler.
- Trust the seasons of your soul.

You learn that winter is not death—it's preparation.
That decay is part of growth.
That nothing blooms all the time, and that's okay.

Nature becomes your mirror.
And slowly, the war inside you begins to still.

Because nature is not trying to be anything but itself.
And when you sit in it long enough, you remember how to be yourself too.

Affirmations From The Earth

"I am one with the cycles of life."
"My roots are deep, my soul is expansive."
"I do not rush—I rise in season."

"The Earth holds me. The wind frees me. The water cleanses me. The fire transforms me."

Narrator's Reflection:
Nature is not just where we go for peace—it is where we *become* peace. In its stillness, we remember the truth: healing does not always come in words. Sometimes, it comes in watching the clouds move, the leaves fall, and the sun rise again without needing permission. The Earth is a quiet teacher, and every time we return to it, we return to ourselves.

40

SOUND AND SONG: THE HEALING POWER OF VIBRATIONS

Long before we had language, we had sound.

The beat of a drum.
The hum of a lullaby.
The chant rising from deep within the chest.
Sound is the soul's first language.

It was there in the womb—your mother's heartbeat, the rush of blood, the soft murmur of her voice vibrating through liquid love. You didn't need to understand words. You felt them.
You were bathed in frequency.

This is why sound, to this day, reaches deeper than meaning.
It bypasses logic.
It touches memory, emotion, spirit.

Because sound doesn't just communicate—it *transforms*.

Vibration Is the Blueprint of the Universe

Modern science and ancient wisdom agree on this:

Everything is a vibration.

- Atoms vibrate.
- Planets hum.
- Your heart beats to a rhythm that matches the Earth's magnetic frequency.

You are not a static being. You are a walking chord, a symphony in motion.

Every cell in your body resonates with energy.
Every thought, emotion, and memory has its own frequency.

So what happens when you introduce sound—pure, intentional sound—into the body?

You realign.
You harmonize.
You heal.

Why Sound Heals So Deeply

Because the body is more of an instrument than a machine.

Think of stress as a note played out of tune.
Think of trauma as a string pulled too tight.
Think of depression as a song forgotten.

Sound—when used with love—can retune the instrument.

When you listen to the right frequencies, sing with your whole chest, or sit in the vibration of a sacred chant, your nervous system remembers balance.
Your body recalibrates.

You don't even have to "understand" the music.
Your body feels it. Your cells know it.

Examples of Healing Sound Traditions

1. Mantras – In Hindu and Buddhist traditions, sacred syllables like *Om* are believed to hold divine frequency. Chanting isn't for volume—it's for resonance. Each repetition aligns the mind and body to higher consciousness.

2. Gregorian Chants – In Christian monasteries, chants were used not just for worship but for emotional stillness. The tonality itself induces meditative states.

3. Singing Bowls & Gongs – In Tibetan and Eastern healing arts, these instruments are used in sound baths to clear blockages, realign chakras, and soothe emotional pain.

4. Drumming – Indigenous tribes worldwide use drumming to connect to ancestors, ground the spirit, and shift states of consciousness. The drum mimics the heartbeat of the Earth.

5. Native Flute & Didgeridoo – Used in Native American and Aboriginal traditions to open the heart and connect with spirit guides. These tones often mimic nature itself—wind, water, animal calls.

Sound is not entertainment here.
It's medicine.

Modern Sound Healing Practices

You don't need a monastery or jungle retreat to experience this. Sound healing is happening in clinics, yoga studios, and living rooms.

Sound Baths:
These immersive experiences allow you to lie back and let sound wash over you. Crystal bowls, chimes, gongs—all vibrating at healing frequencies.
People often cry, release, or fall into deep meditative states.

Binaural Beats:
When two slightly different frequencies are played in each ear, your brain "hears" a third frequency. This entrains brainwaves for calm, focus, or deep sleep.

432 Hz Music:
Unlike the standard 440 Hz, music tuned to 432 Hz is believed to resonate more naturally with the universe, creating harmony in the body and mind.

Voice Toning:
Using your own voice to hum, chant, or tone. This isn't about sounding good—it's about feeling vibration inside your chest, bones, and belly.

Singing As Self-Healing

You were born to sing.
Not just professionally.
Spiritually.

Singing Is A Release.
It clears stuck energy in the throat—the chakra of truth and expression.
It moves emotion through the body.
It creates vibration from within.

That's why you feel lighter after singing in the shower, belting in the car, or humming a tune.

Your voice is an instrument of liberation.

Sing your sadness.
Sing your gratitude.
Sing your longing, your praise, your joy, your confusion.

Even if no one else hears it—your spirit does.

The Relationship Between Emotion And Sound

Sound is the shape of emotion.

- Anger sounds sharp and loud.
- Sadness sounds slow and low.
- Joy sounds bright and full.

When you suppress emotion, your vibration stagnates.

But when you let it express—through voice, music, or sound—you free yourself.

That's why a sad song can bring catharsis.
That's why dance floors feel like church.
That's why a gentle hum can calm a crying baby or a frantic adult.

Sound moves what language cannot reach.

Sacred Daily Sound Practices

1. Start the Morning with a Sound Prayer
   Hum *Om* three times. Or whisper a phrase that resonates, like "Peace begins in me."
   Feel the vibration in your chest.

2. Create a Healing Playlist
   Curate music that lifts your frequency. Let it be your medicine when moods shift.
   Use headphones and close your eyes—let it bathe you.

3. Voice Release at Night
   Before bed, sit quietly. Hum, chant, or sing whatever

sound comes.

Let your body choose the note. Don't perform. Just release.

4. Speak Blessings into Water
   Water absorbs sound. Before drinking, speak healing words into it. "Thank you. I am whole. I am healed." Then drink your prayer.

5. Use Tuning Forks or Apps
   There are tools that emit specific frequencies for healing. A 528 Hz fork, for example, is known as the "Love Frequency." You can place it near your heart or temples.

Affirmations Through Sound

"I am a song sung by the Divine."
"My voice is sacred. My silence is sacred."
"Every cell in me vibrates with healing and harmony."
"Sound carries my intention to every corner of my being."

Narrator's Reflection

You don't have to be a singer to carry a sacred sound. Your heartbeat is a rhythm. Your breath is a tone. You *are* music. The more you tune into your vibrations—the more you sing your truth, listen to healing tones, and honor the medicine of silence—the more you remember who you truly are: a sound born from light, still singing itself whole.

41

WHEN YOU'RE TRIGGERED: RETURN TO THE BREATH

Triggers are teachers dressed as trouble. They arrive uninvited—unexpected flashes of rage, panic, defensiveness, or deep sorrow. Sometimes they look like a simple text. A certain tone. A facial expression. And suddenly, you're somewhere else: not in the present, but in a memory. Not responding, but reacting.

The breath, however, is always here. Always now. Always honest.

When you're triggered, the mind wants to sprint—to defend, to attack, to retreat. But the breath? It calls you home.

Understanding The Trigger

A trigger is not a weakness. It is the soul's alarm system. It says: "There's something here that still hurts."

Triggers are often rooted in:

- Childhood wounds

- Past betrayals
- Fears of rejection, abandonment, or inadequacy

They flare up when a present moment echoes a past pain. But instead of punishing ourselves or others for the reaction, we can use the trigger as a doorway to awareness.

The breath becomes your flashlight in the dark.

The Physiology of Being Triggered

When triggered, the body moves into fight-or-flight. The heart races. The muscles tighten. The breath becomes shallow and rapid.

In that moment, you are no longer in control of your higher mind. You've shifted into survival mode.

But the breath is the bridge. By consciously shifting the breath, you signal safety to the nervous system. You tell your body: "We are not in danger." And when the body believes it is safe, the mind begins to follow.

Returning To The Breath: A Step-By-Step Guide

1. Pause and Notice
   "I'm triggered." Just naming it disarms shame and begins awareness.

2. Inhale Deeply Through the Nose
    Count to 4. Feel the air enter your belly, not just your chest.

3. Hold the Breath
    Count to 4. Rest in the stillness. Let it interrupt the chaos.

4. Exhale Slowly Through the Mouth
    Count to 6 or 8. Let the exhale be a release. Picture the

tension leaving your body.

5. Repeat 3–5 Rounds
   You will feel your heart rate slow, your jaw soften, your shoulders drop.
6. Speak to Yourself Kindly
   "It's okay to feel this."
   "I am safe now."
   "I choose peace."

This moment doesn't need a reaction. It needs your presence.

Breathwork Practices for Trigger Recovery

- Box Breathing (4-4-4-4): Inhale 4, hold 4, exhale 4, hold 4. Great for restoring calm.
- Alternate Nostril Breathing: Helps balance brain hemispheres and emotional response.
- Sighing Exhales: Take a big inhale and let out a loud sigh. Repeat three times to instantly reduce stress.

Use these when:

- You're overwhelmed by an argument
- You get bad news
- You're about to enter a tough conversation
- Your body feels unsafe without reason

Let breath be the intervention before your inner child takes the wheel.

Transforming The Trigger Through Compassion

Imagine this: A child is scared. They lash out. Do you yell back? Or do you kneel, open your arms, and say, "I've got you."

Your triggered self is that child. Instead of silencing it, ask:

- What do you need right now?
- What are you afraid of?
- How can I hold you through this?

The breath gives you the space to choose compassion over control.

The Breath As A Spiritual Practice

In nearly every spiritual tradition, the breath is sacred:

- In Hebrew, the word for spirit and breath is the same: *ruach*.
- In Sanskrit, *prana* is both breath and life force.
- In Christianity, the Holy Spirit is described as the breath of God.

Breathing is not just biology. It's communion. Each inhale is a chance to receive. Each exhale, a chance to let go.

When triggered, you're not broken. You're being invited back—to the breath, to the now, to the self beneath the reaction.

Affirmations To Anchor During Triggers

"I return to my breath. I return to my power."
"I am not the emotion—I am the awareness holding it."
"With each breath, I soften. With each breath, I reclaim."

Narrator's Reflection

The trigger is not the enemy. It's the flare that says, "Look here." And the breath? It is the rope that pulls you back to shore. Inhale grace. Exhale control. Return again, and again, and again. Because peace isn't the absence of being triggered. Peace is knowing where to go when you are.

42

HEALING THROUGH SERVICE AND STILLNESS

There are two rivers that lead to healing: one flows outward, the other inward.

Service is the outward stream. Stillness is the inward one.

Both cleanse. Both nourish. And when we allow ourselves to walk in both waters, we become whole.

The Call To Serve

Service isn't about being perfect. It's not about fixing people. It's about presence.

To serve is to say: "I see you." "I'm with you." "You matter."

And in that simple exchange, healing flows in both directions.

Often, our own pain softens when we hold space for another. Our perspective widens. Our sense of isolation lifts.

Helping others does not mean losing yourself. It means expanding yourself.

It's easy to get lost in our own storm. But when you hand someone else an umbrella, you realize—you were holding one all along.

The Healing Science Of Service

Studies show that acts of kindness:

- Boost serotonin (the "feel-good" neurotransmitter)
- Reduce cortisol (the stress hormone)
- Increase lifespan and overall well-being

Whether it's volunteering, mentoring, listening, giving time or resources—serving others lights up parts of your brain associated with joy, connection, and purpose.

You don't need a title to serve. You don't need a stage, a platform, or perfection.

You just need a willing heart.

Hold the door. Cook a meal. Write a letter. Listen longer. These small acts ripple.

You become the medicine.

Stillness As A Sacred Counterbalance

Yet while service heals outwardly, stillness repairs inwardly.

Stillness is not the absence of movement. It is the presence of awareness.

We live in a world addicted to noise and productivity. But the soul speaks in silence.

When we stop, we hear it: The whisper of intuition. The nudge of truth. The echo of the divine.

Stillness restores the nervous system, lowers blood pressure, and helps the mind reset.

More than that—it makes room for spirit.

Creating A Stillness Practice

1. Begin with Breath
   Before you seek stillness outside, find it inside. Inhale deeply. Exhale slowly. Let the breath anchor you.

2. Designate a Space
   Find a corner, a cushion, a bench outside—wherever you can return to regularly. Make it sacred.

3. Commit to Daily Silence
   Start with 5 minutes a day. Sit. Breathe. Listen. Not for answers, but for awareness.

4. Release the Need to "Do It Right"
   Stillness is not a performance. If your mind wanders, gently return. It's the return that is the practice.

5. End with Gratitude
   After each still moment, whisper thanks: for the breath, for the moment, for the presence.

The Dance Between Doing And Being

Healing does not happen in only one direction.

- When you serve, you offer your energy to the world.
- When you're still, you receive energy back.

This is the sacred inhale and exhale of spiritual wellness.

Too much service without stillness leads to burnout. Too much stillness without service can become detachment.

But together? They become a rhythm: Love in motion. Wisdom in rest.

Service In Everyday Life

You don't need a nonprofit to serve. You just need presence.

- Speak a kind word to the barista.
- Help a stranger load groceries.
- Send a text that says, "You crossed my mind."
- Be a safe space in a conversation.
- Tip a little more than usual.

These aren't acts of charity. They're acts of alignment. They tune your frequency to grace.

Stillness In Everyday Life

- Pause before answering that email.
- Sit in your car for 60 seconds after parking.
- Turn off the music and drive in silence.
- Lay on the grass and feel the Earth hold you.

Stillness doesn't require a retreat. Just a return.

A return to presence. A return to self. A return to Source.

Healing Through Balance

If your spirit feels frayed, ask:

- Have I been giving without pausing?

- Have I been resting without sharing?

Both are sacred. Both are necessary.

Healing is not just about escaping pain. It's about creating wholeness.

And nothing creates wholeness like a life that both *serves* and *surrenders*.

Affirmations

"I give with love and receive with grace."
 "My stillness is sacred. My service is holy."
 "I am not here to fix the world, but to love it, moment by moment."

Narrator's Reflection
You don't have to choose between the hands that help and the heart that rests. Healing is found in both. Let your life be the offering. Let your breath be the altar. Let your presence be the prayer.

Serve when called.
Be still when needed.
Both are enough. Both are love.

43

TRANSCENDENCE, TRANSFORMATION, AND ETERNAL AWARENESS

There comes a point in every soul's journey when the questions shift. From "How do I fix my life?" to "What am I here for?" From "Why did this happen to me?" to "What am I becoming because of it?"

This is where healing becomes transcendence.

Transformation is not just about recovery. It's about resurrection.

Eternal awareness is the space beyond identity, beyond form, where you remember—you were never just a body, a name, or a role. You were light wrapped in experience. A soul having a sacred collision with time.

Transcendence Is The Letting Go Of Labels

You are not your trauma. You are not your title. You are not your income, your weight, your status, or even your thoughts.

Transcendence begins when you stop defining yourself by what was taken from you—or what you've gained.

You begin to witness life, rather than wrestle with it. You move from reaction to realization. You stop trying to "become" and start remembering who you've always been.

Transformation: The Sacred Burn

The caterpillar does not grow wings. It dissolves.

Inside the cocoon, it unravels into formless goo. It becomes nothing—before becoming everything.

So too with you.

Real transformation feels like loss. Like confusion. Like standing in the ashes of everything you thought you were.

But this death of the false self is not the end. It is the beginning of flight.

You must be willing to let the old you grieve... so the new you can breathe.

Eternal Awareness: Living From The Soul, Not The Wound

When you touch eternal awareness, you no longer measure time in days—but in depth. You live from essence, not ego. You understand that every person is a mirror, every event a messenger.

You see yourself in others. And you love them not because they deserve it—but because you've tasted the truth: we are all One.

Eternal awareness brings peace. Because it frees you from the illusion that you are ever truly separate, unloved, or unseen.

You are always held. You always have been.

How To Touch The Transcendent

- Meditate beyond the mind. Sit with the breath until the thoughts soften and you meet the silence that watches them.

- Study the mystics. Read the words of Rumi, Teresa of Ávila, the Tao Te Ching, the Upanishads. Let their timeless truths stir your memory.

- Surrender control. Allow life to move without needing to manage it. Trust that the current knows where to carry you.

- Forgive radically. Release not just others—but the versions of yourself you've outgrown.

- Be present with beauty. A flower. A sunset. A child laughing. These are portals. Step through them.

Affirmations of the Transcendent Self

"I am not in this pain. I am the awareness holding it."
"I am not becoming. I am remembering."
"I am the breath, the silence, the witness. I am whole."

Narrator's Reflection
The deepest healing isn't loud. It doesn't shout or strive. It arises in stillness. In awe. In surrender. Let yourself be undone. Let yourself be held. You are not alone on this path—you are the path.

44

TRUST—THE LEAP WITH NO NET IN SIGHT

Trust is not logical. It's not mathematical. It's not earned by proof.

It is a heartfelt decision. A soul declaration.

Trust says: "I will step even when I can't see the floor." It's the leap made with trembling legs and an open heart.

And sometimes, the floor doesn't appear until midair.

Why We Struggle To Trust

Because we were let down. Because we were hurt. Because the past gave us every reason to stay guarded.

But healing asks something wild: To love again. To believe again. To walk forward without needing the entire blueprint.

That is trust.

It's not blind. It's brave.

Trust Is the Soil of Miracles

Where there is no trust, nothing grows. Where there is trust, everything blooms.

Trust is fertile ground for:

- Peace
- Clarity
- Deep connection
- Manifestation
- Divine timing

When you trust life, you align with its rhythm. When you resist it, you suffer its flow.

Practicing Trust in Everyday Life

- Trust your intuition.
  That quiet voice? It's your compass.

- Trust the process.
  Even the detours are part of the design.

- Trust your healing.
  You are farther along than you think.

- Trust the Universe.
  It's not against you. It's trying to show you something.

- Trust yourself.
  Especially when you feel unsure. That's when faith is real.

Affirmations To Anchor Trust

"I trust that what's for me will not miss me."
"I trust the timing, even when it's slow."
"I trust myself to rise, again and again."

Narrator's Reflection
To trust is to fly without wings. It is to believe in wind before it carries you. Trust doesn't guarantee the outcome—but it transforms the journey. Let go. Leap anyway. Love anyway. You are more held

45

THE MIRROR OF RELATIONSHIPS—HOW OTHERS REVEAL US TO OURSELVES

Every person we meet is a mirror. Not always a clear one. Not always a gentle one. But a reflection nonetheless.

The way we react to others—how we love, judge, cling, or push away—says more about our inner world than theirs.

Relationships are not random. They are assignments. Sacred contracts. Catalysts for growth.

They reveal:

- What we crave.
- What we fear.
- What we've healed.
- What we've hidden.

The Law Of Reflection

When someone irritates you, ask: "What part of me is being touched?"

When someone inspires you, ask: "What quality do I admire that lives—perhaps dormant—inside me?"

When someone wounds you, ask: "What unhealed story is this triggering?"

And when someone loves you deeply, ask: "Am I ready to receive the version of me they see?"

We often think people bring pain into our lives. But more often, they awaken pain that was already there.

Romantic Relationships: The Deepest Mirrors

Romantic love has a way of pulling our shadows to the surface. The vulnerability. The fear of loss. The old attachment wounds.

We think we're fighting our partner. But often, we're fighting our past.

We recreate patterns:

- To prove something.
- To heal something.
- Or to replay a story we never finished.

True love doesn't just feel good. It feels honest.

And honesty is sometimes uncomfortable. But it's sacred.

Friendships And Family: Mirrors Of Growth

Who you choose to be around reflects how you view yourself.

If you surround yourself with critics—you may be echoing an inner judge. If you keep rescuing others—you may be avoiding saving yourself.

Likewise, healthy friendships reflect your evolution. When you grow, your circle often shifts. And that's not rejection. That's the resonance.

You don't need to cling to every connection. Some people were meant to be a bridge—not a destination.

Honor the role they played. Release with love.

Boundaries: The Mirror Of Self-Worth

What you tolerate reflects what you believe you deserve.

Boundaries are not walls. They are mirrors.

They show you—and others—how you value your time, energy, and peace.

You teach people how to treat you by what you allow. By what you reinforce. By what you accept.

Setting a boundary is an act of self-respect. It says: "I see me." "I value me." "I protect my peace."

Healing Through Relationships

You don't have to run from hard relationships. You just have to be conscious of them.

Ask yourself:

- What is this person here to teach me?
- Am I being reactive or reflective?
- What does my discomfort reveal?

You don't heal by avoiding people. You heal by learning through them.

But learning doesn't mean staying in toxicity. Sometimes the lesson is how to walk away.

Other times, it's how to stay present without losing yourself.

Everyone Is Your Teacher

The difficult coworker teaches patience. The gossiping neighbor teaches discretion. The kind stranger teaches compassion. The ex who broke you teaches boundaries.

Each one shows you something. Not about them. About you.

Life doesn't give you perfect mirrors. It gives you cracked ones. Distorted ones. Ones that show just enough truth for you to begin the work.

The Inner Mirror

Ultimately, all relationships are a reflection of the one you have with yourself.

If you abandon yourself, you'll accept abandonment from others. If you distrust yourself, you'll project distrust everywhere. If you love yourself, you'll attract and nurture love.

The world becomes more peaceful when your inner world becomes more healed.

Affirmations For Mirror Work

"I bless the people who reflect my growth."
"I see my triggers as invitations to heal."
"I attract what I believe I deserve—and I am worthy of a healthy, sacred connection."

A Mirror Exercise

1. Sit before a mirror. Look into your own eyes. Not critically. Curiously.

2. Whisper affirmations. Say: "I forgive you." "I see your effort." "I love you."

3. Watch your reactions. What surfaces—tears? Laughter? Shame? Witness it all.

4. Commit to showing up. Promise your reflection that you won't abandon them again.

This is how we shift our outer world—by becoming conscious within the inner one.

Narrator's Reflection
Every relationship is a doorway. Some lead to joy. Some to pain. All lead to truth. Use what you see in others as a sacred map—not for judging, but for growing. The more you understand what others reflect, the more clearly you see your soul.

And in that clarity, you find peace—not because others changed, but because you did.

46

LOVE AS LAW — THE HIGHEST COMMANDMENT

Love is not a suggestion. It's not a mood. It's not a fleeting spark or a poetic phrase.

Love is law. The original code embedded into the soul of the universe. The root of all healing. The engine of every transformation.

When every spiritual tradition is boiled down, love remains the core:

- "Love your neighbor as yourself."
- "Do unto others as you'd have them do unto you."
- "Compassion is the highest virtue."
- "God is Love."

It is not a metaphor. It is instruction. Love is the practice that unlocks peace. The path that returns us to who we really are.

Love As The Essence Of Being

You are not separate from love. You were made of it. You came from it. You return to it.

Everything else—fear, pain, judgment—is learned. Love is what you were before the world began whispering other things.

When you strip away every label, every trauma, every story... What remains is love. That's not romantic fluff. That's the spiritual truth.

The Commandment That Holds All Others

The greatest spiritual teachers didn't give long lists. They pointed to the heart.

Christ said, "Love God with all your heart, soul, and mind... and love your neighbor as yourself." He said every law, every prophet, every teaching hinges on that.

Because if you love fully, you won't harm. You won't steal. You won't betray. You won't remain silent in the face of suffering.

Love regulates behavior not by fear—but by truth.

How Love Heals

- Love dissolves shame.
- Love restores the soul.
- Love repairs the nervous system.
- Love opens space for change.

When someone feels truly loved, they don't need to earn worth. They don't need to compete. They don't need to pretend.

They remember.
That's what love does: it helps us remember who we are before the world gives us reasons to forget.

Love Is A Choice, Not A Transaction

We've been conditioned to trade love: "I'll love you if you love me." "I'll love myself when I'm better."

But real love says: "I love because I am love."

It's not blind. It's awake.

It sees the wounds, the flaws, the shadows—and chooses connection anyway. Not out of need, but out of truth.

Practicing Love as Law

1. Start with self-love.
   Not ego. Not indulgence. But care, honor, compassion. If you can't offer it to yourself, you'll weaponize it with others.
2. Let love interrupt you.
   Pause before reacting. Ask: "What would you like to say here?" Sometimes love says no. Sometimes love says go. Always, it moves with truth.
3. Speak love fluently.
   Say "I see you." "I'm sorry." "I appreciate you." Say the words that restore and realign.
4. Love those who challenge you.
   They are your final exam. Can you hold space for even them? That doesn't mean enabling harm. It means not becoming what hurts you.
5. Forgive in love.
   Not because they deserve it. Because you deserve peace.

What Love Is Not

- Love is not codependency.

- Love is not enabling.
- Love is not perfection.
- Love is not control.

Real love has boundaries. Real love respects individuality. Real love liberates.

If it costs you yourself, it's not love. It's an attachment dressed up as care.

The Ripple Effect Of Love

When you love:

- You calm rooms.
- You soften hearts.
- You shift dynamics.
- You make healing feel possible.

Love doesn't always change others. But it always changes you.

And that's enough to begin shifting the world.

Affirmations of Love's Law

"I was created by love, through love, for love."
"I choose love even when I'm afraid."
"My love is a force—not a weakness."

Narrator's Reflection

Love is not soft. Love is not weak. Love is the fire that burns away illusion.

When you live by love—not by fear or revenge or survival—you become unshakeable. You don't need everyone to understand you. Or like you. Or even agree with you.

You just need to love. Because that is the law. And that is the truth that sets you free.

47

PRESENCE: THE ONLY PLACE GOD LIVES

We often search for God in the distant past or the far-off future. We seek in places of perfection and grandeur, in temples and mountains, in ancient texts and visions.

But what if God is not somewhere else? What if God is not in the tomorrow you are hoping for? What if God is right here?

At this moment.

In this breath.

In the stillness of now.

The Power Of Now

The present moment is the only true space where divinity can be experienced. It's not a philosophical idea—it's the truth embedded in your being.

In every religion, mystics and sages speak of now.

- In Buddhism, there's the concept of *mindfulness*—the practice of being fully present in each breath.
- In Christianity, Jesus said, "Do not worry about tomorrow; let tomorrow worry about itself."
- In Islam, the concept calls for full trust and presence in God's will.

God does not live in your past regrets or your future fears. God lives in the now.

And if you want to find that divine presence, you must be willing to meet it where it is. Right here. Right now.

The Distraction Of Time

Time is an illusion, a construct we've created to make sense of our lives. But the moment you start focusing on the past or future, you miss the eternal truth of now.

The past is just a collection of memories. The future is only a projection.

But the now? The now is real. It is where life unfolds. It is where grace touches you. It is the only space God exists.

When you live in the past, you are holding on to what was. When you live in the future, you are chasing what might be. But when you live in the present—you let go of control and let life unfold.

This is where faith lives. This is where peace is.

Presence As The Path To God

When we think of finding God, we often imagine some grand spiritual achievement. But the divine is already here. Waiting for you to simply notice.

God's presence is in the air you breathe. It's in the quiet moments when your heart beats in rhythm with the universe. It's in the stillness between thoughts. It's in the loving glance you share with a stranger.

Presence is the key to experiencing God as both immanent and transcendent.

The beauty of the moment is that you don't need to search for God—just stop and look around. Stop and listen.

In the silence of now, you will find the presence of the divine.

How To Practice Presence

1. Breathe deeply
   Inhale with full awareness. Exhale with a gentle release. Feel the breath of God entering you.

2. Pause often
   Before speaking. Before reacting. Before rushing ahead. Pause to check in with the present moment.

3. Anchor yourself in your body
   Feel the earth beneath you. Feel your feet on the ground. Feel your heartbeat.

4. Embrace stillness
   Don't fear silence. Silence is where the divine speaks loudest.

5. Let go of the need to control
   You can't control the present moment—but you can choose to fully inhabit it.

6. Listen with intention
   Listen to the sounds around you—birds, wind, the hum of the earth. These are the whispers of the divine.

The Power Of Stillness

In stillness, the divine is fully revealed.

There's a reason why silence has been revered in every spiritual tradition. In stillness, the soul touches eternity. It's in that moment between thoughts where you feel the pulse of life. It's in the silence between words where you hear the truth of your being.

God does not shout. God whispers. God's voice is not a booming thunder—it's the quiet pulse of your own heart. It's the gentle breeze that kisses your face in the morning.

Stillness does not mean inaction. It means the willingness to sit without distraction. To just *be*. To open your heart to what is.

Living From Presence

When you live from the place of presence, everything changes.

- You act with purpose instead of impulse.
- You speak with intention, instead of reaction.
- You listen with compassion, not judgment.
- You respond with love, not fear.

Presence is where true transformation happens. It's in the present moment that you shed the old and step into the new. The past no longer defines you, and the future no longer holds you hostage.

The only thing that matters is right here, right now.

This is where life unfolds. This is where love lives. This is where God dwells.

Affirmations For Presence

"I am here. I am now. I am whole."
 "I release the past and future to embrace the present."

"I trust that God is present at this moment."
"Presence is my portal to peace."

Narrator's Reflection

Presence is the highest form of prayer. In the now, all things are made new. In the now, you meet the divine face-to-face. You are not waiting for God to show up. God is waiting for you to show up to God.

So show up. Right now. In this breath. At this moment. In this sacred *now*, you will find what you've been searching for.

And when you stop searching, you will discover you were never lost.

48

SURRENDER IS NOT DEFEAT—IT'S DIVINE ALIGNMENT

Surrender. For many, it's a word that stings. It sounds like giving up. Quitting. Losing.

But in the language of the spirit, surrender is not defeat. It is the moment when the soul aligns itself with something greater. It is the brave act of letting go—not because you've failed, but because you finally trust.

The Illusion Of Control

We're taught from a young age to strive. To hustle. To hold on tight to what we've built, what we've earned, what we think we deserve.

Control becomes our religion. If we can just manage every variable, anticipate every twist, we'll be safe… right?

But control is a myth. It's a thin veil we stretch over our fear. And it works—until it doesn't.

Until the call doesn't come. The deal falls through. The diagnosis changes everything.

Then what?

Then comes the invitation: Let go. Not because you have no choice—but because you're finally ready to live differently.

Surrender As Sacred Alignment

Surrender is not passive. It's not collapsing into hopelessness. It's an active release. A conscious offering.

It's saying: "I don't know the path, but I trust the One who does." "I don't have all the answers, but I trust the process that's unfolding."

To surrender is to choose divine alignment over egoic control. To open your hands and say, "Lead me."

The Myths We Must Unlearn

- Myth: Surrender means weakness.
  Truth: Surrender takes more strength than resistance.

- Myth: Surrender is giving up.
  Truth: Surrender is giving over—to wisdom higher than yours.

- Myth: If I let go, I'll lose everything.
  Truth: What's meant for you will never miss you. What's not will never stay.

What Happens When You Surrender

- You stop forcing things.
- You begin flowing with life.
- You become more available to grace.

- You sleep better, breathe deeper, love freer.

And sometimes—miraculously—things fall into place. Not because you manipulated them... but because you finally got out of the way.

How To Practice Surrender

1. Acknowledge what you can't control.
   Make a list. Say it aloud. Accept it.

2. Breathe into the unknown.
   Let uncertainty be your teacher, not your tormentor.

3. Affirm your trust.
   "Even this is part of the plan."
   "I am safe, even here."

4. Release daily.
   Before bed, say: "I release what I carried today. I surrender it to something higher."

5. Be willing to be led.
   Open your heart. Pay attention to nudges, synchronicities, and signs.

Spiritual Traditions And Surrender

- In Christianity, surrender is exemplified in the words of Jesus: "Not my will, but Yours be done."
- In Islam, the very name means "submission"—not as punishment, but as peace.
- In Buddhism, detachment is the doorway to freedom—letting go of attachment to outcome.

Every faith honors surrender as a virtue. Not because it's easy—but because it frees the soul.

The Peace On The Other Side

When you stop clutching control like a lifeline, your hands become open enough to receive.

And what you receive is peace. Not peace from the absence of problems—but peace that doesn't require their absence.

Peace that says: "I am guided." "I am held." "I do not walk alone."

Affirmations For Divine Surrender

- "I surrender what I cannot carry."
- "I trust that life is unfolding for me, not against me."
- "Let Thy be done, in perfect time and harmony."
- "Surrender is my strength."

Narrator's Reflection
To surrender is not to lose. It is to win in a different way.

Not with power, but with peace. Not with answers, but with alignment.

You were never meant to carry everything. You were meant to participate in the flow.

Let it move through you. Let grace catch what you release.

In surrender, the soul finds its rightful rhythm. And in that rhythm—you are free.

49

THE EXPANSION OF AWARENESS

Awareness is the first light of transformation. It is the subtle, silent shift that turns reaction into response, fear into curiosity, and unconscious patterns into conscious choice.

When awareness expands, life doesn't change all at once—but your *experience* of life does. The color sharpens. The moment deepens. The patterns that once controlled you become visible. And what you can see, you can shift.

What Is Awareness?

Awareness is not thinking. It is the *observer* behind the thought. It is the presence that watches your emotions rise, without being swallowed by them. It's the inner light that says, "Ah, there it is again"—whether it's anger, anxiety, or joy.

Every spiritual tradition teaches that awareness is sacred:

- In Hinduism, awareness is called *Chit*, one of the three qualities of the Supreme (Sat-Chit-Ananda).
- In Buddhism, awareness (*sati*) is the foundation of mindfulness.
- In Christianity, Jesus repeatedly asked his disciples to "stay awake."

Awareness is the beginning of awakening.

Levels Of Awareness

1. Self-Awareness:
   Noticing your own thoughts, feelings, and patterns without judgment. "I'm feeling tense right now." "I tend to react this way when I feel rejected."

2. Relational Awareness:
   Noticing how your presence impacts others and how others reflect parts of you. "I see that I withdraw when others get close."

3. Environmental Awareness:
   Becoming attuned to the energies, sounds, colors, and beauty around you. "The light in this room affects my mood."

4. Spiritual Awareness:
   A growing recognition of your connection to something greater—God, Source, the Divine. "There is more here than meets the eye."

What Expands Awareness?

- Stillness: You can't hear subtle wisdom when the noise is too loud.
- Journaling: Writing slows the mind, revealing patterns and insights.

- Meditation: Watching the mind teaches you how it moves—and how to quiet it.
- Contemplation: Deep thinking on sacred texts, quotes, or personal questions.
- Nature: When you spend time in natural spaces, awareness opens naturally. Trees don't rush. Rivers don't apologize.

From Judgment To Observation

Awareness expands when you move from judging yourself to *observing* yourself.

You don't need to fix everything in a moment. You just need to *see* it.

- Instead of "I'm so dramatic," try "Wow, I have a lot of emotion right now."
- Instead of "I'm lazy," try "My energy feels low today—what's beneath that?"

Observation is curiosity without criticism. It is the foundation of transformation.

Awareness Dismantles Illusion

The stories we tell ourselves lose power when held in the light of awareness.

"I'm unlovable." "I'm not safe unless I control everything." "I have to prove myself to matter."

When you *see* the story, you can question it. When you question it, it begins to loosen.

Awareness breaks the trance. And in its place, truth begins to rise.

Living With Expanded Awareness

When Your Awareness Expands:

- You no longer chase every thought like it's the truth.
- You begin to pause before reacting.
- You notice how others reflect your inner landscape.
- You find stillness in moments that once triggered chaos.

Expanded awareness is not about perfection. It's about presence. It's about seeing more clearly, loving more fully, and choosing more wisely.

Affirmations For Expanded Awareness

- "I am the witness, not the wound."
- "Every moment is a doorway to greater clarity."
- "What I observe, I can heal."
- "I release judgment and choose curiosity."

Narrator's Reflection

Awareness is not the end of the path. But it is the light that guides every step forward.

With awareness, you no longer move through life blind. You walk with your eyes open, your heart attuned, your soul listening.

And in that clarity—in that gaze that sees beyond surface and fear—you awaken to the truth:

You were never broken. You were just becoming aware.

And now... you are free.

50

THE ART OF BEING—WHERE DOING ENDS AND BEING BEGINS

We live in a world obsessed with doing. To-do lists. Productivity hacks. Goals, achievements, hustle.

But there comes a moment in every soul's journey where doing isn't enough. Where accomplishment feels empty. Where motion without meaning becomes noise.

And it's at that moment you're invited into the sacred art of *being*.

Doing Is The Outer Dance. Being Is The Inner Music.

You can build the business. You can raise the children. You can save the world.

But if you forget to *be*—to feel, to breathe, to rest in your own presence—you will lose the thread.

Being is not passivity. It's presence. It's the state of existing with such depth, such clarity, that even stillness feels alive.

Why Doing Feels Safer Than Being

Because doing is measurable. You can count it. Track it. Get praise for it.

Being? It's invisible. You can't show it off. You can't rush it. You have to *surrender* to it.

For the ego, that feels terrifying. But for the soul, it is home.

Being Doesn't Mean You Stop Living. It Means You Start Living Fully.

- Doing says, "What's next?"
- Being says, "What's here?"
- Doing asks, "What should I fix?"
- Being asked, "What wants to be felt?"
- Doing runs.
- Being listened to.

When you practice being, your doing becomes more meaningful. More rooted. More aligned.

You no longer perform. You embody.

Practicing The Art Of Being

1. Sit Without a Goal
   Just sit. No phone. No book. No plan. Feel what it's like to simply exist.

2. Do One Thing Slowly
   Wash a dish. Fold a towel. Pour tea. Slowly. Mindfully. With presence.

3. Notice the Space Between Tasks
   Pause before jumping to the next thing. Let silence speak.

4. Journal Without Prompt
   Let your inner self pour onto the page without direction. Just being, in words.

5. Let Yourself Be Witnessed
   Sit with someone who sees you—and allow yourself to be seen. No mask. No explanation.

Being As The Portal To God

God doesn't rush. Spirit doesn't hustle.

Being is where the eternal meets the now. It's where breath becomes prayer. Where existence becomes enough.

All the sages, prophets, and mystics knew this. That the highest spiritual frequency is not found in grand gestures, but in deep presence.

To be is to touch the face of God.

The Gift Of Being In A Doing World

You are not your tasks. You are not your achievements. You are not your schedule.

You are a living soul. A divine expression. A presence capable of shifting the energy of any room—not by effort, but by essence.

Your being *is* your blessing.

Affirmations For Sacred Being

- "I am not what I do. I am who I am."
- "This moment is enough. I am enough."
- "I return to my presence, where all peace lives."

- "In stillness, I remember my essence."

Narrator's Reflection

At the end of the road, no one remembers how many emails you sent or deadlines you met.

What lives on is how you make people *feel*. How deeply you loved. How present you were.

Being is the bridge between your spirit and this moment.

So rest. Breathe. Return.

Because in the art of being, you stop striving for life... and start receiving it.

And that is where the journey truly begins.

51

SUFFERING AS A SEED—THE GROWTH THAT BEGINS UNDERGROUND

Suffering is often misunderstood. We run from it. Hide it. Curse it. But in the quiet wisdom of spiritual truth, suffering is not a punishment. It's a planting.

A sacred seed. A buried invitation. A hidden root of future strength.

Every tree was once a seed, buried in darkness, pressed by soil, pushed by storms. And so were you.

Why Suffering Feels Like The End

Because it *hurts*. Because it strips away certainty, safety, identity. It humbles the ego. It exposes the illusions we clung to. It breaks the shell so the soul can breathe.

The caterpillar dissolves into nothing before it becomes the butterfly. You are not breaking. You are becoming.

Suffering Awakens Us

- To what really matters.
- To who we really are.
- To the depth we didn't know we had.

You can't fake your way through pain. It demands presence. It strips away the performance. It makes you look in the mirror of your soul.

The Underground Season

Growth doesn't start when people see it. It starts underground. In the quiet. In the dark. In the seasons nobody applauds.

When you feel buried, remember: You've been planted. And what grows in darkness often blooms in light.

Trust the unseen. Trust the silence. Trust the seed.

Not All Pain Is Punishment

Sometimes pain is protection. Sometimes it's preparation. Sometimes it's the only thing strong enough to wake us up.

Think of all the awakenings that didn't happen until the heartbreak. Until the betrayal. Until the loss.

We don't wish for suffering. But when it comes, we can let it shape us. Not with bitterness—but with deep, sacred growth.

Suffering As Sacred Alchemy

Pain becomes power when it's held with presence. Grief becomes grace when it's breathed through. Loss becomes light when it's offered to love.

You don't need to rush out of your pain. You need to *sit* with it. Speak to it. Ask what it's here to teach you.

The soul doesn't waste suffering. It transforms it.

Practices For The Underground Season

1. Name your pain honestly.
    "This hurts. I feel abandoned. I feel confused."

2. Breathe into it.
    Don't resist the feeling. Let breath soften the edges.

3. Write letters to your future self.
    From the seed. From the soil. From the struggle. One day, that version of you will thank this one.

4. Trust the timing.
    Roots take time. So does healing. Don't rush your bloom.

5. Invite divine companionship.
    You are never suffering alone. Let your prayers be raw. Let God meet you there.

Affirmations For The Season Of Suffering

- "This is not the end of me. This is the planting of me."
- "Something sacred is growing beneath what I can see."
- "I trust what is forming in the dark."
- "I do not rush the seed. I honor its becoming."

Narrator's Reflection

You will look back one day and say: "That season almost broke me... but it built me."

Because the roots that grow underground are the ones that keep the tree standing in storms.

You are not forgotten. You are not failing. You are being formed.

And what emerges from this sacred soil— will be stronger, braver, more radiant than you've ever known.

Because suffering doesn't shrink you. It *grounds* you.

And from that ground...

You rise.

52

GRACE OVER GUILT—THE PATH OF RETURNING WITHOUT SHAME

We've all fallen. Missed the mark. Let ourselves down.

But shame was never meant to be our spiritual home. Guilt may knock on the door, but *grace* is what opens it.

Grace is the bridge back to yourself. Back to God. Back to peace.

Not because you earned it. But because it was never withheld.

The Weight Of Guilt

Guilt is the soul's alarm system—it tells us we've strayed. But when it lingers too long, it becomes shameful. And shame isn't corrective. It's corrosive.

Shame says: "You *are* the mistake." Grace says: "You made a mistake—and you're still worthy."

To live under guilt is to wear chains God never put on you. To live under grace is to walk in freedom God always had waiting.

Return Is Always Possible

There is no detour so far that you can't return. No failure too deep. No moment too late.

Grace doesn't ask if you've cleaned up your life. It asks if your heart is ready to come home.

The prodigal son wasn't met with a lecture. He was met with a robe. With a feast. With a father who ran.

That is how heaven greets return.

Why We Struggle With Grace

Because we think love must be earned. Because we grew up with conditional approval. Because religion sometimes taught us more about punishment than about mercy.

But true spirituality is not about rule-keeping. It's about relationships. And in every real relationship, forgiveness is part of the rhythm.

You don't have to crawl back. You can *run* back. Because grace runs faster.

Practicing Grace For Yourself

1. Speak gently to your past self.
   Use the voice you wish someone had used with you.

2. Remember who you are, not just what you did.
   Actions may disappoint—but identity is sacred.

3. Replace punishment with presence.
   Instead of beating yourself up, sit with the lesson. That's how you grow.

4. Extend grace to others.
   The more you forgive, the more you understand the miracle of your own forgiveness.

5. Let grace define your next step.
   Not fear. Not guilt. But grace. Always graceful.

Affirmations For The Return Journey

- "I am not my mistake. I am God's miracle."
- "I walk in grace, not guilt."
- "I return with my whole heart—and that is enough."
- "Shame is a lie. Grace is the truth."

Narrator's Reflection

You were never meant to carry that weight forever. You were never meant to prove your worth.

You were meant to *receive* love. To *remember* your holiness. To *return*—as many times as needed.

Because grace isn't running out. It's rushing in.

And it's calling you not to perform, but to come home.

Not with your resume. But with your heart.

And in that holy return, you are not punished. You are embraced.

You are not condemned. You are crowned.

Welcome back.

53

DIVINE TIMING—TRUSTING THE UNFOLDING

There is a clock beyond our clocks. A rhythm deeper than deadlines. A timing not built by man, but by the Divine.

This is divine timing—the sacred unfolding of life according to Spirit's wisdom, not our own. It rarely matches our expectations. But it always matches our evolution.

Why Divine Timing Feels Frustrating

Because we are taught to rush. Because society values speed over surrender. Because we confuse delay with denial.

But what if the wait is not punishment… But protection? What if the slow season is sacred? What if what's being prepared for you requires the preparation of *you*?

Divine timing never withholds what's meant for you. It only aligns it when *you* are ready to receive it fully.

The Illusion Of Control

We love to plan. To plot. To organize the future like it owes us predictability.

But faith begins where the illusion of control ends. When we stop trying to force outcomes and start trusting what's unfolding.

Because Divine wisdom sees what we don't. Not just the destination—but the terrain. Not just the prize—but the process.

How To Live Aligned With Divine Timing

1. Let go of forced timelines.
   Your worth is not measured by your speed.

2. Honor the season you're in.
   There is a reason for the quiet. There is a reason for the momentum. Both are divine.

3. Trust the pauses.
   Some doors don't open because what's behind them is still being built.

4. Align your actions with peace.
   Do what you can from a place of flow, not force.

5. Watch nature.
   A tree doesn't bloom in winter. Neither should you. Everything blooms when it's time.

What Divine Timing Teaches

Patience. Presence. Humility.

It teaches us to move in rhythm with grace. To act when nudged—not when panicked. To pause when the Spirit says wait—even when the ego says go.

It teaches that waiting doesn't mean wasting. And being still doesn't mean being stuck.

Affirmations For Trusting The Unfolding

- "What's meant for me cannot miss me."
- "I am on time, even when I feel behind."
- "Divine wisdom orders my steps."
- "I rest in the rhythm of sacred timing."

Narrator's Reflection
We've spent so long racing that we've forgotten how to receive. So long that we've forgotten how to flow.

But grace doesn't follow your schedule. It follows alignment.

And in that place—where you stop chasing and start trusting—you realize: You were never late. You were being led.

Because what is *for* you is not in someone else's hands. It's in divine hands.

And those hands are never rushed. But they are never wrong.

So breathe. Return. Trust the unfolding.

You are not behind. You are being *perfectly guided*.

54

THE WATCHER—YOU ARE NOT YOUR THOUGHTS

If you can observe the thought, you are not the thought. If you can name the feeling, you are not the feeling.

There is a part of you that watches. Witnesses. Hold awareness without judgment.

That part of you is the soul. And that is your power.

The Illusion Of Identification

Most of us live trapped in a storm of thoughts. Worry. Judgment. Regret. Planning. Fear.

We believe those thoughts define us. We say, "I am anxious." But more accurately: "I am *experiencing* anxiety."

You are not the cloud. You are the sky. You are not the noise. You are the awareness underneath it.

The Role Of The Watcher

The watcher doesn't argue with the mind. It doesn't try to stop thoughts from appearing. It simply notices.

"I see you, thought." "I hear you, fear." "I feel you, grief."

And in that noticing, something shifts. The thought loses its grip. The emotion becomes manageable.

Because now... you are the observer. Not the reactor.

Practicing The Watcher's Seat

1. Name what arises.
   "I notice tension in my chest." "I'm having the thought that I'm not enough."

2. Create distance.
   Use phrases like, "My mind is telling me..." instead of "I am..."

3. Return to the breath.
   The breath is the anchor. The observer's refuge.

4. Visualize the sky.
   Let each thought be a cloud drifting by. Don't chase them. Don't hold them. Just watch.

5. Journal from the watcher's voice.
   Write as the soul—not the ego. Let stillness speak.

Freedom Through Awareness

The moment you realize you are not your thoughts, you reclaim your peace. You don't need to fight the mind. You need to *watch* it.
Awareness is not passive. It is powerful. It brings choice. It invites clarity.

When you watch without clinging, you disarm the patterns that have ruled you.

Affirmations For The Watcher Within

- "I am not my thoughts. I am the awareness behind them."
- "My mind is active, but I am still."
- "Thoughts come and go. I remain."
- "I observe. I witness. I choose."

Narrator's Reflection
You've spent years believing everything your mind told you. Every fear. Every doubt. Every self-judgment.

But now... you've remembered the watcher. The quiet one inside. The one who sees with love. Who listens without panic. Who watches—and in watching, brings light.

Your mind will still speak. That's its nature.

But now you'll know: you don't have to believe it all. You don't have to become it all.

You can return to the seat of stillness. And watch the storm pass.

Because you are not the storm. You are the sky.

55

THE RETURN TO WHOLENESS

You were never broken. Just buried. Covered in pain, expectation, conditioning.

But beneath all of it—still intact—is your wholeness. The soul never shatters. Only the story does.

And this is the invitation: To return. To reclaim. To remember who you were before the world told you otherwise.

What Fractures Us

Trauma. Shame. Betrayal. Unmet needs.

These aren't just emotional events—they're identity disruptions. We begin to believe we *are* the pain. We lose access to the innocent one, the empowered one, the divine one.

But pain is not the end of the story. It's the beginning of the return.

The Illusion Of Brokenness

You don't need fixing. You need *uncovering*. Like Michelangelo said of David: "I saw the angel in the marble and carved until I set him free."

That is your journey. Not to become someone else. But to *free* who you've always been.

What The Return Looks Like

1. Facing the fragments.
   Healing doesn't mean pretending everything's fine. It means meeting what's not.

2. Reclaiming the exiled parts.
   The angry child. The fearful teen. The silenced adult. All are welcome home.

3. Listening without judgment.
   Your wounds are messengers, not mistakes.

4. Trusting the soul's memory.
   Deep down, you *know* your wholeness. You've just been distracted.

5. Integrating through love.
   Not control. Not perfection. Love.

Signs You're Returning To Wholeness

- You react less, reflect more.
- You feel more grounded in your body.
- You stop chasing validation.
- You remember your power.
- You stop waiting to be saved—and begin walking yourself home.

Affirmations For Wholeness

- "I was never broken—only buried."
- "All parts of me are welcome."
- "Wholeness is not a destination. It's my true nature."
- "I return to myself with love."

Narrator's Reflection

Wholeness was never out there. It was never in a relationship. Never in a title. Never in perfection.

It was always in you. Waiting. Whispering.

Now, the layers are peeling back. The noise is softening. And what remains is *real*.

Your truth. Your light. Yourself.

Not a new you. But the *true* you.

Welcome home to your wholeness. You never really left. You only needed to remember.

56

LIVING AS LIGHT—BECOMING A BEACON FOR OTHERS

You don't have to preach to shift the atmosphere. You don't have to lead a movement to start a wave.

Just *be light*. Live with love, presence, and authenticity. And the world around you will feel it.

What It Means To Live As Light

To live as light is not to be perfect. It is to be *anchored*. To carry clarity in confusion. Peace in pressure. Love where there has been lack.

Your presence becomes a balm. Your energy speaks before your mouth ever does. You begin to reflect something deeper than logic— something sacred.

This is not about performance. This is about alignment.

Light doesn't *try* to shine. It simply *is*.

Why It Matters

Because someone is watching. Someone is weary. Someone is wondering if peace is even possible.

And when they see you—calm in the storm, soft in the battle, steady in the unknown—they remember.

They remember who *they* are.

When you become light, you remind others they're not alone. You become the mirror they forgot they needed.

The Path To Becoming A Beacon

1. Do your inner work. You can't share what you haven't experienced first. Heal. Reflect. Grow.

2. Live with integrity. Say what you mean. Mean what you say. Let truth be your rhythm.

3. Lead with love. In the silence. In the room. In the choices no one sees.

4. Protect your peace. Light isn't loud—it's consistent. Guard your energy.

5. Shine through service. Not for validation, but as overflow.

The Ripple Effect Of Radiance

You'll never know who was healed by your honesty. Who was comforted by your kindness. Who kept going because they saw you rise from your lowest.

Light spreads without effort. It multiplies without permission.

When you become a living example of alignment, the world takes notice—even if it never says a word.

Affirmations For Living As Light

- "I don't chase influence. I carry light."
- "My life reflects love, peace, and power."
- "Wherever I go, healing follows."
- "I am a mirror for others to see their own light."

Narrator's Reflection
We often underestimate the power of simply *being*.

But light doesn't shout. It doesn't compete. It just shines.

And that quiet brilliance is enough. Enough to shift a room. To calm a heart. To awaken a soul.

So live as light. Walk in your truth. Stand in your peace.

You never know who needs your glow to find their own. But trust this: Your light matters. And the world is brighter because of it.

57

BEYOND THE MIND, INTO THE HEART OF GOD

There is a knowing beyond words. A peace deeper than logic. A truth wider than belief systems.

It does not live in the mind. It resides in the heart.

To reach it, you must descend—not climb. You must feel—not figure out. You must surrender—not strive.

This is the doorway into the heart of God. And it opens not with intellect, but with intimacy.

The Limits Of The Mind

The mind is a tool, a servant, a lens. But it cannot hold the totality of the divine. It asks questions love has already answered.

God is not a riddle to be solved. God is a presence to be *entered*.

And for that—you must go beyond thought. Beyond theology. Beyond the boundaries of belief.

Into the mystery. Into the heartbeat. Into the stillness where love speaks without sound.

The Language Of The Heart

The heart listens differently. It doesn't debate. It doesn't dissect.

It *receives*. It *feels*. It *remembers*.

This is why the mystics weep without reason. Why the awakened often seem undone. Because the closer you get to God, the more you realize—you were never separated.

Living From The Heart Of God

1. Trust what doesn't make sense. Faith begins where formulas fail.//
2. Open yourself to wonder. Let awe break the walls of certainty.
3. Let love be the compass. Not religion. Not rules. But love—pure and unfiltered.
4. Return to simplicity. Breath. Presence. Connection. These are sacred.
5. Feel everything. Avoid nothing. Pain is not a punishment. It's part of the passage.

The Heart Knows What The Mind Forgets

It knows the sacred is not in control—it's in surrender. It knows the goal was never perfection—it was presence. It knows healing doesn't come from fixing—it comes from loving.

In the heart of God, there are no tests. Only invitations. To return. To remember. To rest.

Affirmations For Heart-Led Living

- "I surrender thought to the silence of truth."
- "I dwell in the heart of God."
- "Love is my guide. Always."
- "What I cannot understand, I will trust."

Final Narrator's Reflection

You've traveled far. Through fear, doubt, silence, stillness, ritual, breath, service, surrender, forgiveness.

You've peeled back the layers. Sat with your pain. Listen to your soul.

And in the end, it wasn't about becoming something new. It was about returning to what you've always been: A soul formed in light. A heart shaped by love. A being capable of carrying God.

Now, you know: Peace isn't found in the absence of struggle, but in the presence of grace within it.

Faith isn't built in answers, but in the willingness to walk with the unanswered.

And love—true love—is not a reward. It's the *source*.

So go now—not as someone searching. But as someone who *remembers*.

You are not lost. You are not late. You are not broken.

You are light. You are loved. You are home.

Beyond the mind. Into the heart of God. Forever.

OTHER BOOKS BY TIERRE FORD

www.ingramcontent.com/pod-product-compliance
Lightning Source LLC
Chambersburg PA
CBHW050339010526
44119CB00049B/610